Educating Children with Facial Disfigurement

Children and young people who are visibly different face significant social and psychological challenges at school. *Educating Children with Facial Disfigurement* demystifies a difficult and delicate subject. Teachers and others working in education can use this book to acquire a better knowledge of the issues involved, as well as the confidence to handle sensitive issues. This book will also help foster inclusive attitudes both in and out of the classroom.

There are many causes which include birthmarks, cleft lip and palate, burns, scars and serious skin conditions, so it is essential that all schools know about the issues arising from visible difference. The author examines many of these issues and shows in a practical way how to deal with:

- Staring, curiosity and answering questions;
- Teasing, name-calling and bullying;
- Medical needs, special educational needs and related issues;
- Creating inclusive school communities;
- Self-perception and self-expression;
- Career ideas and work experience;
- Social skills for life.

With illustrative case studies, and reference to useful resources, this book will be of particular relevance to teachers with responsibility for special educational needs or pastoral care. It will also provide insight for health professionals working with school-age children and parents of children with a facial difference, and anyone with a commitment to inclusion.

Jane Frances is a Consultant to the School Service at Changing Faces, UK.
Special Educational Needs

Educating Children with Facial Disfigurement

Creating Inclusive School Communities

Jane Frances

RoutledgeFalmer
Taylor & Francis Group

LONDON AND NEW YORK

First published 2004 by RoutledgeFalmer
11 New Fetter Lane, London EC4P 4EE

Simultaneously published in the USA and Canada
by RoutledgeFalmer
29 West 35th Street, New York, NY 10001

RoutledgeFalmer is an imprint of the Taylor & Francis Group

© 2004 Jane Frances

Typeset in 10.5/12pt Bembo by
Graphicraft Limited, Hong Kong
Printed and bound in Great Britain by
TJ International Ltd, Padstow, Cornwall

British Library Cataloguing in Publication Data
A catalogue record for this book is available from the British Library

Library of Congress Cataloging in Publication Data
A catalog record has been requested

ISBN 0-415-28045-1

Never doubt that a small group of thoughtful,
committed citizens can change the world.
Indeed, it is the only thing that ever has.

Margaret Mead

Contents

Figures

Tables

Acknowledgements

In addition to the people acknowledged in the text, I am vastly grateful to:

... my wonderful colleagues at Changing Faces for tolerating my distraction and supporting me throughout this project ...

... the children and young people, and their parents, whose experiences, anecdotes, inventiveness, tenacity, and generous readiness to share, are largely responsible for this book ...

... the teachers with whom I have worked, some closely, some distantly, for nearly six years as Changing Faces School Specialist, who have wanted to make things better in school for pupils with disfigurements.

Introduction

Figure 1.1 Playing together begins with looking and being looked at (see pp. 18–19)

A widespread 'first lesson in disfigurement' occurs on the bus or in some other public place at around 3 or 4 years old. At that age we're forever pointing things out to the grown-up we're with, asking questions . . . Then, 'Hey!' we point – 'Look at that man! Why is his nose like that?' Suddenly, instead of the patient, informative answers we've learnt to expect, we're being told in harsh, urgent whispers not to stare.

How might this sort of lesson affect us?

Option A

For the adult who has the child with them . . .	*For the child who only asked . . .*
They pass on what they themselves were taught as a child in a similar situation . . .	The child is interested and curious . . .
The child is badly behaved for asking such a loud, rude question . . .	This grown-up doesn't know the answer . . . and is annoyed about being asked . . .

The child's bad behaviour is embarrassing or annoying . . .	I'm being told off but it's not my fault. It must be that man's fault, the one with the interesting nose . . .
I can't seem to control my child. Really it would be easier if this man who looks different were not on the bus at all.	It's all gone wrong. Horrible man.

In future, having a go at someone whose appearance makes us stare will be an obvious and attractive option.

Option B

For the adult they are with . . .	*For the child* . .
The adult is concerned to protect the *unfortunate* man with the unusual nose from further embarrassment . . .	The first time this happens it is a question – the child is interested and curious . . .
How hard it must be to live with such a face . . .	It's terrible to have a face like that . . .
We must always be kind and protect such unfortunate people by averting our gaze.	Whenever I see anyone who looks different like that, I must turn away and think about something else.

Whenever s/he subsequently encounters someone who looks different, this child will try to avoid interacting with them.

An unspoken lesson in difference (observed on the concourse at a London railway terminal)
A family are waiting, with all their luggage, for their train: father, mother, son, daughter. They glance up at the departures board and exchanged a few words with each other. The father and son wander off, perhaps in search of refreshments. The mother and daughter, a fair-haired girl of about 7 with a little fair-haired doll, are left sitting among the luggage.

After a minute or two, one of the many pigeons wandering about on the concourse comes closer. The pigeon is lame – it has one proper pink pigeon foot but its other leg ends in a little pink stump. The mother turns away to stare long and hard at the departures board. The little girl stares long and hard at the pigeon as it pecks and limps, pecks and limps, just beyond their luggage. The mother continues earnestly to study the departures board. Suddenly the little girl jumps up and waves her doll aggressively at the lame pigeon, which jumps backward and then hurries unevenly away.

If saying 'Don't stare' and saying nothing are not helpful, what would be better? See pp. 23 and 29.

Who this book is for

Looking different, having a disfigurement – particularly when the face is affected – makes it very hard to lead a normal life. One in 500 children are affected,[1] and a further 1 in 100 has a noticeable facial disfigurement or other noticeable feature. Children who are visibly different are more prone than their peers to depression, anxiety, emotional, behavioural and cognitive problems, and social isolation. They tend to have fewer friends, fewer vocational aspirations, and they underachieve at school.[2] The most commonly expressed concern of these children and young people themselves are other people's reactions – embarrassment, staring, turning away, comments, questions, and teasing. But it needn't be like this . . .

This book is for those involved in the education of all these children and young people. It aims to provide both information and practical support strategies concerning the *social* challenge of disfigurement, disability and 'visible difference'. With so few pupils affected, it can be difficult to acquire the knowledge and experience needed to work effectively with a pupil who has an injury or condition that affects the way they look.

Although disfigurement may affect only one or two pupils in a large secondary school, in another sense it is part of a much wider concern that affects many more at every school – appearance per se. Among 'ordinary teenagers' between 11 and 16 years old:[3]

- 94 per cent had appearance concerns
- 51 per cent specifically cited fear of teasing or bullying about appearance
- 31 per cent said lack of confidence about appearance affected academic work
- 20 per cent of Year 9 pupils (13 to 14 years old) claimed to truant because of perceived poor appearance.

This book is also about creating inclusive school communities where every member of the increasingly diverse population can feel more positive and self-assured about appearance, and can develop and enjoy their own and each other's positive qualities as individuals.

Having an injury, illness or condition that affects the way you look

There are many conditions and injuries which affect appearance. A child may have been born with a condition such as cleft lip, Apert's, Moebius, or a port wine stain. They may have acquired scarring or lost fingers through burns, dog bites and other traumatic injuries. Conditions such as eczema, vitiligo, acne and haemangioma are not usually present at birth but appear in infancy or childhood. A child's appearance may have been altered by illness or its treatment, as in leukaemia. Some conditions, such as loss of an eye, are permanent and relatively stable. Lymphangioma, eczema, vitiligo, haemangioma and many others are more variable. Children's speech, hearing, and in some cases eyesight, may be affected by their disfiguring injury, illness or condition.

Medical treatments range from major cranio-facial surgery, through laser treatment, to ongoing management. Plastic surgery can often make conditions less conspicuous but complete transformations are very rare, and for many disfiguring conditions no effective treatment is available.

People who look different are in a

> strange half-way position in terms of being handicapped. Someone with facial disfigurement isn't handicapped in the same way as a person in a wheelchair, for example. And yet as a disfigured person you are socially handicapped because of your odd-looking face.[4]

'When the stigmatized person's failing can be perceived by our merely directing attention (typically visual) to him . . . he is likely to feel that to be present among normals nakedly exposes him to invasions of privacy.'[5]

Disfigurements of the face or hands are particularly noticeable, and disfigurements affecting the eyes-mouth 'communication triangle' tend to be especially unsettling for others. But other parts of the body will also be on show at times. Summer clothes, swimming and getting changed for sport can trigger curiosity or staring, even from good friends and familiar classmates. Conditions such as cerebral palsy or scoliosis, affecting a child's posture or movement, may also trigger curiosity in others which resembles social reactions to facial disfigurement.

> Attitudes, expectations and reactions are more favourable toward attractive adults and children. Attractive individuals are perceived and treated as more popular, more likeable and morally better than less attractive individuals. Peers, parents and teachers are all more attentive, responsive and warm toward attractive children . . . Infants with facial disfigurement receive less physical contact and less expressive interaction with their parent and the quality of infant-parent attachment is not infrequently impaired.[6]

People with disfigurements

> are subjected to visual and verbal assaults and a level of familiarity from strangers not otherwise dared: naked stares, startled reactions, "double takes", whispering, remarks, furtive looks, curiosity, personal questions, advice, manifestations of pity or aversion, laughter, ridicule and outright avoidance. Whatever form the behaviours may take, they generate feelings of shame, impotence, anger and humiliation in their victims.[7]

The social psychology of appearance and difference – what seems helpful versus what is helpful

Working with people with facial disfigurement in particular and visible difference in general is full of strange surprises. What you think you should do, out of kindness and good intentions, to help a pupil who looks different may not improve things at all. Something you think you should not do because, for instance, you don't want to increase the self-consciousness of the affected child, may turn out to be the most effective intervention of all. This book draws extensively upon research into the social psychology of appearance and visible difference, and upon careful evaluation of a range of support strategies undertaken in many different schools.

For instance, it might seem that children with the most severe disfigurements will be the most seriously adversely affected. But research shows, on the contrary, that a person may be seriously affected by their unusual, changed or changing appearance, even though it does not look so very bad to you or others.[8] This may be because reactions to a minor disfigurement are less consistent, whereas responses to a major disfigurement are more predictable. Or because those with a minor facial defect are more likely to be laughed at than those with a severe impairment, who may well evoke pity.[9] However slight the appearance anomaly seems to us, we cannot help a pupil by telling them it isn't very noticeable.

Nor can we hope that pupils will somehow 'grow out of' the difficulties they are experiencing. On the contrary, dislike of a child with a facial disfigurement increases with age: older children tend to be less accepting.[10]

Table 1.1 Well-meant advice to children with facial disfigurements

Child/young person complains . . .	Well-intentioned adult responds . . .	Desired goal . . .	Likely outcome for child . . .
'Everyone keeps staring at me.'	'I expect you're imagining it.'	That the child with a disfigurement can can go through life without being too troubled by other people's reactions.	Child feels alone with this difficulty.
And yet . . .	If adult sees another child staring: 'Don't stare. It's rude.'	As above.	Other children turn away. Child feels s/he must be repellent.
'They keep calling me names and won't let me play.'	'Just ignore them.'	As above.	Child feels alone with this difficulty. Adults lack knowledge and power.
'I'm scared of what will happen when I go to my new school.'	'You'll be fine. After all, no-one here ever notices or says anything.'	As above.	Child starts new school with no strategies to deal with all the new people's reactions to how they look so is powerless and distressed by questions and staring.
'I'm bored. I haven't got anything to do.' Or persists in making conversation with adult, e.g. on playground duty.	'Go and play. Look – I'm sure Jo and Sam will let you play ball with them.'	That child can join in and have some fun, unhindered by appearance concerns.	Child tries but fails to 'join in'. Becomes still more lonely and anxious.
Other children ask, 'What's the matter with her face?'	'That's not a very nice question. We're all the same underneath. It's the person inside that counts.'	To help the other children to ignore differences and be more inclusive.	Devalues everything adults say about difference. Increases curiosity and speculation because of difficulty in obtaining information.

A school may therefore attempt to be warmly and genuinely inclusive by requiring and insisting that everyone is to be accepted just for who they are. But even though we may not consciously intend to treat another differently or less favourably when they have a facial disfigurement, almost all people do, especially upon first meeting them.[11]

When out and about, and whenever they must meet someone new, the child or young person who looks 'different' will be acutely aware of other people's initial surprise at their unusual appearance. In the absence of specific understanding and practical strategies for dealing with other people's reactions, the person who 'looks different' is left struggling with all the unwanted attention they are subject to. This can lead to disruptive or (bizarrely) 'attention seeking' behaviour on the part of the stared-at child or young person. 'They appear to be inviting negative responses from adults for their behaviour, which they can control, rather than for their appearance, which they cannot.'[12] Or it can lead a child to reject social situations, including school.

The extent of the staring and loss of anonymity experienced by people of all ages (and by the families of babies and small children) who look different, should never be underestimated. Rather than 'ignoring' (saying nothing, pretending we don't notice, etc.), the most effective strategies are, in fact, those which either internally or aloud acknowledge what is going on – strategies which *do something*. A simple verbal response, for example, along with suitable body language, can enable others to move beyond their initial, disconcerted reaction. *Having something to say* in response to other people's reactions takes courage, time and practice. School is a very important social environment and therefore a good place, with help and support, to undertake this learning task.

Research into other disabilities or differences often highlights more practical difficulties requiring a combination of political will and practical provision to overcome them. With much campaigning, these improvements have at last begun to accrue – better advocacy for people with learning difficulties, more accessible public transport for people with restricted mobility, signing at theatres for people with impaired hearing . . . In the same spirit, projects are set up to enable young people with all kinds of disabilities and differences to participate in a wide range of stimulating activities. But 'support workers appeared to concentrate on involving [these young people] in activities [whereas the young people themselves] . . . clearly conveyed that their priority was to develop relationships, make new friends and hang out with established friends. Activities were enjoyed and appreciated but did not appear to be the main event.' Because of this, for young people who are 'different', the quality of time spent out of school depended on relationships with other young people in school.[13] This book is about increasing 'social access' for people who are vulnerable to being seen as 'different'.

In many schools where staff have used *Changing Faces* approaches to support a pupil with a facial disfigurement, the feedback has included the finding that other pupils have benefited too – pupils with other kinds of special needs or disabilities, and pupils with no obvious 'special needs'. Specific advice and coaching around social skills, and strategies for managing uncomfortable or vulnerable feelings when among peers, have led to unexpected gains in social confidence. When the social skills and anti-bullying approaches specifically developed for use by children with facial disfigurements were taught to whole year groups of pupils in secondary school, perceived levels of bullying decreased by almost two-thirds from 58 per cent to 21 per cent.[14]

People, both 'them' and 'us', need both a positive self-perception and inclusive social skills in order to move comfortably and confidently from seeing someone as 'different' to engaging with all kinds of different people as people, and finding out what we may have in common with each other. This book promotes researched and evaluated approaches to 'difference' which are positive and inclusive for all concerned.

Language

Some writers (particularly when addressing medical aspects of disfigurement such as causes and treatments) are very specific: 'Deformity refers to a condition which is in some sense congenital . . . Disfigurement . . . refers to a condition which has been acquired.'[15] Others are more concerned about the impact of a word on those who hear it, particularly the impact upon children to whom a word maybe applied – 'as a group we found the term "facial disfigurement" too harsh, cruel even, so we prefer to say "facial difference".'[16]

Words are important. The words used, especially by someone with authority such as a teacher, educational psychologist or doctor, can affect the child in ways which are both subtle and profound. When a teenage girl became so self-conscious about her facial asymmetry and so sensitive to other people's comments that she stopped going to school, it was eventually discovered that the specialist who had diagnosed her scoliosis had told her it was a *deformity* she'd had since birth (see p. 89). Another pupil whose cheek was seriously scarred after being bitten off by a dog, felt terribly hurt when a teacher told him (probably with some affection) 'Don't be cheeky'.

Using euphemism for a child's appearance can imply some kind of 'taboo'. Direct, objective language makes it easier to talk about things. But children and young people can benefit greatly from opportunities to consider a wide range of words and phrases. When they are ready, they can choose how to describe themselves and their appearance with words that are both meaningful and comfortable. This is fully explored in Chapter 2. But it is mentioned here to explain the decision to vary the terminology throughout this book.

> Disfigurement . . . facial difference . . . distinctive feature . . . unusual skin . . . unusual-looking . . . noticeable . . . visible difference . . . interesting face. . .

Phrases which link or separate how a person looks from the person who looks like that also need some thought. For example, is a person with a facial disfigurement a disfigured person? On the one hand it seems important to distinguish between a person's appearance (which may be different, disfigured, scarred, affected by eczema, distinctive, etc.) and a person's person. So 'person with a disfigurement' might be preferred to 'disfigured person'. On the other hand, the way we look – the face we have – is a key aspect of our identity. Having a disfigurement can hugely affect a person's identity and place in society. Being visibly different, disabled, disfigured, is stigmatizing. In Erving Goffman's unsurpassed book *Stigma*[17], people's subjective experience is explored and the terminology is surprising and challenging – 'When stigmatized [people with disabilities] and normals [non-disabled people] do in fact enter one another's immediate presence . . .'.

Another area where language can jar is where text or speech is quoted which seems less than respectful towards people who are different. For example K.H. Rubin and

M. Wilkinson, in their compelling 1995 work on peer rejection and social isolation in childhood,[18] write that 'Children without developmental delays tend to exhibit low acceptance of mentally retarded peers'. They reference this aspect of peer rejection to research published by Wallander and Hubert in 1987. So 'mentally retarded' may just be 'old-fashioned' terminology. 'I don't belong in here with these low-grades', quotes Goffman again.

It is important to notice when vocabulary, terminology or language irritates or jars or seems unhelpful or wrong. Awareness of this phenomenon can help staff to support a child or young person more effectively.

Inclusion, change and action

Placing a child with special educational needs in a mainstream environment used to be called *integration*. The opposite would be segregation – generally into a different building, reached by a different bus. How does *inclusion* differ from integration? A clue is that its opposite – exclusion – can happen in the same classroom without a chair or desk being moved, and, at home-time, it can happen inside the same bus closely surrounded by all the other mainstream pupils.

The Warnock Report[19] tackled the 'medical model' and highly medicalized 'treatment' of children with disabilities. Before then, children were allocated to categories such as 'educationally sub-normal' (ESN) and spent their childhood in special units (often nice places) attached to hospitals. With Warnock came the new idea of Special Educational Needs (SEN): all children were located on a continuum of need, some having a higher level of need than others. They were all to be educated within a mainstream environment where possible. (In the USA, the 'mainstreaming' of handicapped children was brought about by a law entitling them to 'the least restricted environment'.) The ideal of inclusion is not new.

The newest legislation makes the requirements of the Special Educational Needs and Disability Act 2001 enforceable by law, overseen by the Disability Rights Commission, whose stated goal is 'a society where all disabled people can participate fully as citizens'.[20] Since September 2002 it has been illegal for any school to discriminate against disabled pupils. Local education authorities and schools must develop strategies and plans to improve accessibility for disabled pupils, over time. 'The Act covers all educational and associated services for pupils and prospective pupils – in essence, all aspects of school life, including extra-curricular activities and school trips.'[21]

As with the Disability Discrimination Act 1995, disability includes severe disfigurement. Pupils who have injuries or conditions that affect the way they look may or may not have special educational needs. At the same time they will often have special psycho-logical and social needs, 'psycho-social disabilities' perhaps, and are often seriously at risk of being socially excluded within the school environment.[22] The psycho-social diffi-culties associated with being visibly different may not be seen as educational needs but may well affect their ability to partake of all aspects of school life. Within the ideal of 'inclusion' expressed by the Disability Rights Commission, there is debate and uncertainty about how inclusive mainstream education works in practice for children who are seen as 'different'. Mainstream education has an inherent 'normality' which shapes the experi-ences of children with SEN and their 'mainstream' peers: 'many mainstream pupils either "tolerated" or "excluded" these children.'[23]

This difficulty lies at the heart of the challenge of social inclusion in schools. There exists a prevailing concept of *inclusion* where the boundary is redrawn wider to bring more groups or individuals inside. Into

> an already given set of procedures, institutions, and terms of public discourse. . . . those [previously] excluded or marginalized are incorporated without change . . . [T]he particular interests, experiences and ways of looking at things that the formerly excluded bring . . . make little difference to [the newly inclusive institution's] processes or outcomes.[24]

Alongside the development of more positive goals for difference and inclusion (diversity), backed up by legislation, political pressure has also been directed, constantly, at *raising standards*. The overriding importance of educational achievement is continually emphasized and has been built into new mechanisms for assessing children's (and their teachers') abilities and attainments. The privileging of curriculum-based achievements and academic excellence can leave educational professionals (and parents) struggling with 'inclusion' *versus* educational attainment. Inclusion demands full participation for everyone. But the already existing curriculum, the means by which newly 'included' pupils are 'supported' in 'accessing' it, and the demands of academic excellence, always risk reducing acceptance to 'tolerance' for any pupil whose 'difference' or 'special needs' means they are not 'mainstream' – and *we all know who they are.*

'The presence of a support worker not only inhibited friendships but also on occasion caused resentment, as other young people wanted time without adults who they saw to be in a supervisory role.'[25]

This book is about increasing social inclusion and reducing social exclusion in schools. Sometimes this means specific extra input or support for children and young people who are vulnerable to being seen as different. Sometimes it means reviewing and altering some of the things we think and do – often quite small things. But above all inclusion must involve all staff and all pupils – to make the social culture of the school more widely and positively inclusive.

Teachers

Teachers, meeting and engaging with their pupils day-in, day-out, with authority and as people, have a key role. This book aims to enable teachers to educate pupils who are visibly different knowledgeably, sensitively and effectively.

If you are not a teacher, imagine for a moment being one. Your pupils' education is brought to life by the quality of your presence, the way you look at and see them, the way you talk to them and listen to them, the way you share your knowledge and expertise, the atmosphere of your classroom, lab or playing field . . . These 'invisible' aspects of your work may appear to have little to do with disfigurement – but appearances can deceive!

Above all, this book is for teachers. The importance of the work they do, and the people they are doing it for, cannot be exaggerated.

Chapter 1

Our beliefs and feelings about disfigurement

Before approaching the education of pupils who look different, it is essential to pause and consider the people – primarily the teachers – whose contribution will be at the core of the inclusive education we want these children to experience.

Being there

After all the rhetoric about inclusion, and after all the to-ing and fro-ing which may have gone on to enable a particular pupil to attend a particular school, perhaps with additional support or other special considerations, the child or young person is there in the classroom. Alternatively, after an absence in hospital and perhaps a period on home tuition, a pupil returns to school with their appearance altered. Finally, it is down to the teacher. In the classroom, with the pupil who is visibly different (there may be more than one), and with all the other pupils who are perhaps more likely to be seen, and to see themselves, as 'normal', the teacher's reactions are crucial. When inclusion begins to be achieved it will be largely because of things teachers do (perhaps without knowing that they are doing them) – the way they engage with their pupils, the individuality they perceive and respond to in each one of them, the futures they imagine for them.

When a teacher believes a pupil is gifted, the impact on the pupil's performance is well established. What about other beliefs about pupils which teachers may hold?

Seeing difference

This is not a discussion about the *idea* of differences and the ideal of inclusion. It concerns the feelings and beliefs about disfigurement we notice and discover in ourselves when we see a child or young person with a disfigurement, or when we watch (during a *Changing Faces* in-service training day for instance) some video clips of young people talking about their experience of living with facial disfigurement.

When we meet someone new, who has a facial disfigurement, their appearance is unsettling . . . for several seconds we are disconcerted, which makes it hard to *meet* the person. This is not *wrong*, it's just what happens.

This unsettling initial attempt at meeting may be coloured by many different feelings and reactions. A teacher may feel embarrassed, shocked, upset, angry, vulnerable or even repulsed by a child whose appearance is unusual, or they may be touched with pity. These feelings can seem quite inappropriate and it can seem natural and right to try and expunge them from our awareness. In fact, an acceptance, internally, of our own initial feelings and reactions is an important part of being real – of not pretending, as the following teachers' accounts clearly show:

> When I visited Jamie in hospital I was so shocked. I don't know what I'd expected but I hadn't expected – I wish I'd been warned, been prepared somehow. I had to kind of pull myself together – saying hello, chatting, giving him the cards his classmates had done. But inside I was going, 'Oh my God. Oh my God.' I don't know how Jamie coped at all – or his parents and his sister. Afterwards I was so emotional – not like me at all.

> When the video cut to another person – who had been in a fire I guess and looked . . . *unusual* – I heard someone giggle. A colleague, obviously. If it had been a class of kids and not a staff meeting I'd have hauled them out and told them off for not showing respect, or whatever. As it was I could see how it was a nervous, embarrassed reaction, not an *amused* giggle – this colleague was mortified, of course. My own reactions? I didn't notice – all I noticed was this giggle. Maybe it was a relief to be distracted – a relief not to have giggled myself.

> The deputy head burst in, very uncharacteristically rattled, and asked me to see this family, complaining quite sharply that they ought to have told him the girl had special needs. He'd left them sitting in his office. It felt very abrupt and awkward – as SENCO [Special Educational Needs Co-ordinator], I would usually do a lot of preparation before meeting a child with their parents. In fact there were no special needs but the girl had a disfigurement. For some reason this didn't disturb me unduly but Bob said later that all he could think of was if something like that ever happened to his own daughter.

> The video clip gave me a lump in my throat. I was glad it was a training session and not someone in my class and me up there at the front having to press on regardless. Though I'm sure I would have coped – putting on the usual professional front, as you do.

With classes to teach and pupils to see to, marking and preparation, plus a hundred other things adding to the general pressure, and an Ofsted inspection coming up fast, teachers may not even pause to register fully their own reactions to a pupil's unusual appearance. It is essential to make the time to do this. It helps us to be real, to recognize and register other people's feelings and reactions, and especially to appreciate the pupil's own feelings about their visible difference and other people's reactions to the way they look. More experienced teachers of children who are visibly different face a similar challenge:

> [if] sensitivity . . . has been lost . . . [and] you no longer react to a disfigured appearance when meeting someone for the first time it becomes impossible to understand the significance of their disfigurement. This can be an issue for more experienced helpers. Some develop a more blunted sensitivity to the appearance and predicament of those in their care.
>
> Choniere *et al.*, 1990 . . . [found that] more experienced nurses [on burns units] underrated the pain when this was compared with patients' own judgements. Less experienced nurses produced closer estimates to those given by their patients.[1]

Beliefs about appearance and disfigurement

People considered physically attractive benefit from wide-ranging social advantages[2] including popularity, success in job interviews, and leniency in courts of law. A brief glance at most magazines and much TV output confirms that being 'good looking' is highly prized. The desire to be good looking has given rise to a whole industry based on beauty products and treatments.

There are many traditions across the world and across time that link goodness to beauty and interpret disability, injury and illness as misfortunes wrought by God, or fate, or ancestors to punish a person or test or teach them in some way. Hospital patients who believe that they have been abandoned by God are at greater risk of death.[3] The best and kindest intentions may lead good Christian people, for instance, to pray for someone's healing – for a miracle, perhaps. Surely, if their life is blighted by a disfiguring condition, illness or injury, they must long to be cured, 'made whole'. Or if not a miracle, then miraculous gene therapy or plastic surgery might help. There has even been a suggestion that whole-face transplants will soon be undertaken.

All these historical, cultural and scientific influences may seem to confirm that disfigurement blights a person's life. In fact it is other people's reactions to disfigurement that are the problem here[4] – the reactions of people who are 'severely normal' as Geoffrey Lay puts it in his difficult book about healing ministries.[5]

> It is the responsibility of future research to determine how best to educate the general public about biases and prejudices that they may have toward the craniofacial patient. The hope is that one day this research will provide the means to change societal attitudes towards craniofacial patients so that they will not have to endure the double burden of considerable social as well as surgical pain.[6]

Through its extensive work with many hundreds of people with facial disfigurement, *Changing Faces* has identified some important misconceptions prevalent among the general public.[7]

'He's so brave'

It is often thought that anyone who overcomes disfigurement is a real hero. Simon Weston, for example, is such an important role model in so many ways, especially – one imagines – for young people with serious burn injuries.

But what if the person with the disfigured appearance does not feel brave? 'I'm not a soldier type at all. I passed my test and crashed my car. Now look at me.'

The reality is that coming to terms with disfigurement, like any other medical condition, is hard and there is little choice to be had. A person with a disfigurement will feel very down at times (as do most people) and there are ways of dealing with difficulties and making headway. The support of family and friends – and school staff and classmates – is often crucial.

'She'll be fine after surgery'

The myth of surgery is often perpetuated by by advertisements for cosmetic surgery and simplistic medical stories which seem to show miraculous 'cures' but often hide scarring with make-up and lighting. It also ignores the important research finding that the severity of a disfigurement (as perceived by others) has no proportional relationship to the social or psychological distress experienced or the adjustments made to it.[8]

The myth can lead to disappointment when expectations of surgery are not met. It can contribute to social difficulties being misconstrued, as when a boy with an unusual-looking blind eye was referred to hospital by his school, suggesting surgery to fit him with a proper-looking prosthetic eye to stop the other children calling him 'one-eye'.[9]

Surgery can be very effective in treating many conditions and advances are happening all the time. However, there are many disfiguring conditions for which no effective treatment is currently available. Medical interventions can rarely remove a disfigurement completely. It is important to be informed, sensitive and realistic regarding surgical treatments.

'He's so scary!'

The myth of horror created by people's fear of the 'unknown' or 'difference' is perpetuated by stereotypical portrayals of evil characters in horror films (and James Bond films, etc.), comic strips and fairy tales as having some sort of disfigurement.

It can lead to people being afraid of anyone who is disfigured or to ridiculing them with names like 'Phantom' and 'Two Face' from popular films.

'Impairment is an ordinary part of human life but it is feared by so many and I remind people of their fear' was how one young man explained his constant rejection by the majority.[10]

In reality, moral character and outward appearances are not linked in any way. The more people with visible differences are seen in public and in the media, at school and at work, in a wide range of roles, just like everyone else, the more ordinary and acceptable disfigurement will be.

'She's got no future'

People sometimes express a view that only normal-looking people succeed, and having a disfigured appearance means having a second-rate life.

There are in fact many people with disfigurements leading full lives, with careers, families, and all the usual ups and downs. Not heroes – just ordinary people. They have developed social skills and strategies, and built up their self-esteem to respond effectively each time they encounter someone who stares or doesn't know where to look, and to overcome negative stereotypes and underestimates of their potential.

> **Check yourself out**
> What do you see when you look at someone? There is their face, of course, their 'looks' – good looking? not so good looking? What about posture, body language, their physical presence? Then there is their self-presentation in terms of what they wear and how they wear it, how they have their hair, if they wear make-up or jewellery . . . How important is appearance for you? Your appearance? Other people's appearance? What does a person's outward appearance say about them? How are you affected by people's appearance?

What do we notice about the children and young people we work with – and our colleagues and everyone else we spend time with? How good are we at registering aspects of personality, character and attitudes, the quality of their eye contact, their energy, sensitivity, imagination or humour?

What about parents?

It may seem to school staff that a parent has somehow contributed or is contributing to your pupil's difficulties at school. Just as it may sometimes seem to a parent that the school is 'to blame' for things that go wrong for their child at school. Having emphasized the importance of the teacher's role for the pupil's well-being at school and beyond, it is important not to underestimate the part played by parents, too, or the challenges they face.

The destination is *different* – that's all

Having a baby is like planning a fabulous trip – to Italy. You buy a bunch of guide books and make your wonderful plans.

There's a host of things to do and see – including the Colosseum, Michelangelo's *David* and the gondolas in Venice. You may learn handy phrases in Italian. It's all very exciting.

After months of eager anticipation the day finally arrives. You pack your bag and off you go. Some hours later, the plane lands.

The stewardess announces 'Welcome to – *Holland*.'

'Holland??' you say. 'What do you mean, Holland?'

'I signed up for Italy! I'm supposed to be in Italy! All my life I've dreamed of going to Italy.'

'But there's been a change of flight plan. They've landed in Holland and there you must stay.'

The important thing is that they haven't taken you to a horrible, filthy place full of famine and disease. It's just a different place.

You must buy new guide books and learn a whole new language – and you will meet a whole new group of people you would otherwise never have met. It's just a different place. It's slower-paced than Italy and less flashy – but after you've been there for a while, you look around and begin to notice that Holland has windmills, Holland has tulips, and Holland has Rembrandts.

But everyone you know goes to Italy and they're all bragging about what a wonderful time they had there. And for the rest of your life you will say: 'That's where I was supposed to go, that's what I planned to do.'

The pain of that will never go away because the loss of a dream is a very significant loss. But if you spend your life mourning the fact that you didn't get to Italy, you may never be free to enjoy the very special, very lovely things about Holland.

(Reprinted with kind permission of CLAPA UK and the Northern Beaches Learning Difficulties Support Group, Sydney Australia.)

A mother describes a shopping trip with her baby daughter, soon after the first operation to repair the baby's bilateral cleft lip: 'My husband was off in some other aisle with the trolley and Maria was sleeping in my arms. Suddenly this woman was shouting, "*I'm going to tell the NSPCC about you, what you've done to that baby.*" Right in my face. I was so shocked. I was so hurt. Angry. Speechless.' (The NSPCC were running a television campaign at the time, to involve the general public in helping to put a stop to violence towards children.) This mother already knew of *Changing Faces* and sought help by talking through her feelings of anger and powerlessness with a telephone counsellor.

> [S]ignals indicating infants' needs may be non-existent or may be 'mixed' due to physiological, sensory or cognitive [difficulties]. In a study of infants . . . with . . . Down Syndrome, brain injury, blindness, or multiple disabilities (any or all of which can be accompanying features of craniofacial handicap) . . . disturbances in one or more attachment behaviours [were found] for *all* infants. Communicative signals such as vocalizations and smiling occurred rarely or were late in developing in most of the infants studied . . . [T]he [parents'] task of *understanding* the infants is extremely difficult.[11]

Parents whose baby has a disfiguring condition face enormous challenges: forming a strong emotional attachment to a new baby who is taken away, examined and operated upon by doctors; overcoming breathing and feeding difficulties (mouth, nose or throat are often affected); guilt, blame, rejection and over-protection. Similar challenges arise when an infant or child is injured or becomes seriously ill – suffering burns for example, or meningitis (which can lead to amputation of hands and feet).

There will be a complex process of grieving for the loss of the hoped-for child or the formerly perfect child who has been damaged by illness or injury. There will be medical consultations and hospital stays, possibly at specialized units many miles from home. There may be prolonged treatments which the child may find hard to endure – the wearing of pressure garments while scars heal, or the creaming several times a day of skin conditions. Siblings may have to stay with relatives, and may feel angry (and guilty for feeling angry) at all the attention paid to their brother or sister – plus bearing all the extra questioning and perhaps teasing they get at school about it. Friends and some family members may feel less comfortable visiting the house.[12]

The wider social and material environment can also seriously influence parents' ability to cope – for example, 'mothers . . . who have social and financial support are less negative in their interactions with their infants'.[13] But it has to be good support.

> My mother used to take Josh out in the pram so that I could get some sleep. She'd cover him right up so that no-one could see his face. She was ashamed. Of course, she didn't say so – it was just another impossible feeling knotted up inside me.

Medical involvement can leave the parent feeling that they are not skilled or equipped for the job they have to do. They may be shown how to carry out special procedures to do with feeding or keeping a tracheotomy clear and open. They may have to take their child back again and again to a hospital where the doctors make him or her cry and cry.

Guilt and distress may lead to indulgence and over-protectiveness. It can take many years, and may need the help of a suitable counsellor, for a parent to accept the way their child is, and to feel that they are a good enough parent.

Then the time comes for the child to start or return to school:

> The first day the mother came in – with the youngster in a pushchair – she got into a fight with a couple of other mums at the gate. It was awful. The child had a large, brown, sort of hairy-looking birthmark on his face and it emerged that the mother just never went out with him because of the way other people stared. So he'd been out of the flat maybe half a dozen times in four years.

A pupil with a disfigurement may become isolated, failing to make friends, or getting teased. They may behave aggressively towards other pupils, or have an unacceptable level of absence from school. There may be ongoing or occasional medical needs that have proved difficult to manage. The parents may ask for a meeting, or the school may invite them in to discuss their child's difficulties.

Meetings can be very big, involving a dozen or more health and education professionals plus staff from the local education office. They

> can be very hard for parents whose child is 'different'. They want their child to be included, to have 'the same' education as all the other children. And yet their child has particular and different needs – as the need for a meeting somehow affirms. [C]ontradictions that arise from education policy and provision, and from the discourse of 'inclusion' . . . and 'tolerance' often result in parents having difficulty negotiating the 'official' process, or constantly 'fighting the system'.[11]

School staff may be greatly appreciated by a parent who found it difficult to see a future for their child. Or a parent may find fault with everything the school does. Some parents of children who have disfigurements may over-attribute negative experiences to their child's appearance, which can help to preserve the self-esteem of a stigmatized group.[15]

> In the end, the thing that really helped was when we found ourselves talking about something else. I was seeing the children off as usual, and bracing for the usual 'How was Sean today?' from his Mum – trying to think of something useful to say. But when I got to the door I saw the traffic outside was solid, and when Sean's Mum arrived I said, 'Have you come from town? Is something going on?' She told me about the burst water main and we talked about what route I'd have to take to avoid it. Then Sean turned up with his coat and they said goodbye and off they went. After that I tried something different every afternoon. Stuff on TV, the weather, the school fair on Saturday . . . Like breaking a habit. Looking back, it's like Sean's Mum needed to say something to me – his teacher – every day – and we both kept talking about Sean. But actually, talking about anything did the job – whatever the job was – just as well. It *felt* like Sean began to relax more, to look back over his shoulder less – but I may be telling myself that to try and make sense of it.

Chapter 2

Having something to say

Figure 2.1 This boy's 'speech bubble' will work much better than 'Stop staring. You're being very rude', when he joins his new classmates (see pp. 22–3)

Staring

All but the very youngest of children – and virtually all adults – will know on some level that 'It's rude to stare'. So when other people stare it will seem that they need reminding that staring is rude and they'd better stop it.

Most people feel and say that discriminating against people who look different is not fair. We try not to do it – perhaps we are *sure* we don't do it. But extensive observation has identified 'behavioural changes in able-bodied people upon first encountering facially disfigured persons'[1] – emotional arousal, gestural activity, duration of eye contact, use of personal space, time spent in face-to-face interaction, anxiety and a 'pronounced stickiness of interactional flow'. Even though others may not consciously intend to treat a person differently or less favourably when they have a facial disfigurement, almost all people do, especially upon first meeting them.[2] When we see someone new who has a disfigurement, we do not look for longer because we are rude – we look for longer because we are human.

Nevertheless, being looked at can feel rude and hurtful. In reaction, the reminder 'Don't stare' may come out as an angry retaliation – and get the child who looks different (or their parent) a negative reputation. Even a polite request, 'You're being very rude – please don't stare', can be counter-productive: new people may turn away or leave the situation. However, studies of the process of 'making friends' (or forming a 'primary dyad') show the importance of looking and being looked at:

Observational dyad → activity dyad → enduring feelings towards
one another → primary dyad[3]

Looking at a child with a disfigurement (observational dyad) is apt to take the form of looking for longer or staring. If this looking/staring is prohibited or interrupted, the youngster who looks different is at risk of social isolation.

And yet being stared at is very unpleasant. Out and about, people with facial disfigurement (and the parents of small children who look different) have no access to the kind of social anonymity or polite disregard which everyone else takes for granted. In the queue at the ticket office others will be having a look at the traveller with the disfigurement, some discreetly, others blatantly. When they get to the window to buy their ticket, the chances are that the sales clerk will stare and falter too before the transaction gets underway. Unwanted attention will dog them throughout their rail or bus journey – 'people wouldn't stop staring at me. So I took my coat off and put it over my head. I couldn't see but it didn't matter. I wished I was never born.'[4]

Most people with facial disfigurement also report comments from complete strangers ranging from (kindly meant?) 'Have you thought of getting help from a plastic surgeon?' to 'People like you should stay at home.'

Parents with an infant or child whose appearance is unusual will see their son or daughter being subjected to these 'typical' reactions.

> You know how people love to go coochy-coo at a baby and they see the pram and in they go for a little peek and – BAM! That look on their face and I just can't believe it doesn't *harm* Grace – getting that look instead of a nice smile. It certainly broke my heart. We had to not go out.

At *Changing Faces* in London, this mother learned two main strategies for going out in public: (a) go with a friend; (b) be prepared to say, 'Grace has a rather large birthmark. It doesn't bother her. If you ping her rattle she'll probably give you a smile.' One day an older woman saw Grace and said, 'Oh, your baby has a naevus. My daughter had one just like that', and gave Grace a huge smile.

Other people's reactions in public places can leave children and young people of all ages, and their parents, feeling hurt and angry. A demoralizing sense of powerlessness can take hold through being unable to stop this happening.

For people whose appearance falls within the 'normal' range, and who are therefore used to other people's inattention in public places, these high levels of unwanted attention and offensive remarks may be hard to imagine or believe.

What is going on?

From the point of view of the person doing the looking, they may well not quite know for the first moments that they are even doing it. Then they realize they are staring, and may turn sharply away in embarrassment. Or they may try to compensate, so to speak, for having stared by offering a well-meant but inappropriate comment. Or, one surmises, they may be influenced by past tellings-off for staring and 'have a go' at the person whose unusual appearance has 'caused' their discomfort. Or, in their confusion, they may come up with something astonishingly patronising. 'I'd gone to cast my vote.

The woman doing the ballot papers spoke to the person I was with. "*Would he like to vote?*" [little voice as if talking to a small child] As if having a disfigured face means all kinds of other mental baggage.'

What's going on here?

A person who is visibly different may be 'unsure' . . .

Others, upon first seeing them, may be 'unsure' too . . .

Feeling		Behaviour	Feeling		Behaviour
unsure	U	uneasy	unsure	U	uneasy
noticeable	N	nervous	nervous	N	nosy
self-conscious	S	shy	surprised	S	staring
upset	U	uptight	unprepared	U	unkind
rotten	R	resentful	repulsed	R	rude
embarrassed	E	edgy	embarrassed	E	escaping

Source: V. Kish and R. Lansdown (2000) 'Meeting the psychosocial impact of facial disfigurement: Developing a clinical service for children and families', *Clinical Child Psychology and Psychiatry*, 5 (4).

In fact, both the person with the disfigurement being looked at and the person looking at them are in difficulties. At some point in the future, the person doing the looking will have grown up in such a diverse and inclusive society and enjoyed such an excellent school education that they will grasp the situation and know just how to behave:[5]

- If you find yourself staring at someone you probably won't see again, smile and nod a small acknowledgement and carry on your way.
- If you find yourself staring at someone you're likely to see around, smile and say 'Hi'.
- If you find yourself staring at someone in the college canteen or at a party, go over and try a bit of conversation – see if you can find any interests or opinions or a sense of humour that you both share.

In the meantime, it is probably the person who has the disfigurement who is going to have the expertise here:

> They are literally scared of the unknown: how can they possibly communicate with you? They've never met anyone like you before and they are scared of talking to you, scared of hurting you, scared of asking questions, scared of looking at you . . . *You* have to help them break out of their 'scared-ness' and meet you face to face.[6]

How to stop staring

There are several approaches for managing encounters with strangers or the awkward initial moments with new people.

Reassure

Use eye-contact and a smile, a passing comment or a low-key phrase to enable the other person to 'see' more of the person whose unusual appearance is all there seems to be. A little information can help – to give the thing a name for instance:

> If you react passively you make [nervous people who are unfamiliar with facial disfigurement] even more uneasy. It may be much better to [say], 'Yes, I was burned, but I'm okay now' – just a few simple words to get the subject into the open. By taking the initiative, you put them at ease . . . It gets easier for you as you become more familiar with other people's initial reactions, but it is always the first time for them.[7]

> Nowadays I usually just say, 'It's okay, it's only a skin condition. You can't catch it.'

> We were in the car stopped at a red light, near this residential place. I've never been there. There were these three – I think they were teenagers – my sort of age – in wheelchairs, with helpers, adults, pushing them. Crossing the road. I was staring – I didn't know I was staring until one of the people in the wheelchair, the middle one of the three – he just heaved up his hand in a sort of wave. It was awkward for him, you could see his muscles or his nerves or something made it physically awkward. But it was a clear message and he was looking right at me. Like, 'Hello, you.' And I waved back, and smiled – I *hope* I smiled anyway. It was like I was staring and I hadn't got a clue, but he was really sharp and sociable and knew how to make it okay. In fact, what went through my mind was, 'I wouldn't mind getting to know you better.'

Humour

James was seriously burned in a car-fire in his teens. His brother recalls:

> I remember going into pubs with you and being aware of conversation stopping and eyes drilling into our backs. In one, you completely disarmed a group of starers with the throwaway comment, 'Not looking my best today, I'm afraid.'

> 'Oh heck,' placing hands urgently over lower face but keeping eyes (smiling eyes) on staring stranger on bus, 'have I put my face on inside out *again*?'

> 'Your attitude to the world has to become more extrovert, so as to convey the message that you are really all right . . . Natural reserve was OK before but it won't bring you much reward now. So take the plunge – what have you got to lose?'[8]

Making first encounters more positive –
Having something to say

The challenge is to convert the new person's startled, uncertain initial reaction – 'unsure' – into a more positive social interaction. This helps the person with the disfigurement to achieve and maintain social confidence. It liberates the other person from 'baggage' about 'difference' (see pp. 13–14) so that they can meet this new, distinctive-looking person properly.

1 Acknowledge, understand and tolerate 'unsure' initial reactions.
2 Inform and reassure – add an aspect of 'inner self' to the outward appearance which gets so much attention.
3 Move the encounter on – 'change the subject'.

This manages the process of being looked at without jeopardizing the chance to get to know new people.

A small child might have just one simple version for when they're new or when a new child joins the class:

> I'm Sam. It's just the way my face is. What's your name? Do you want to play football?

A seasoned practitioner knows how to take the lead and vary their approach to suit each occasion:

> Hi. You must be Jacki. I'm Sol. Don't mind my face – think of it as modern art if you like. Shall we get a coffee and look at these estimates?

Showing a parent and small child how this can work for them

When a 5-year-old with facial scarring was being prepared to take up her place at a large primary school after three years in a very small kindergarten, part of a special preparatory session went like this:

> The special visitor had a teddy. It was badly scorched. Amy was interested straight away, saying something about the 'strange fur'. Then the bear read from a little card it was holding – '*Stop staring at me, you're being very rude.*' The bear was clearly cross. Amy was quite put out by that, and turned sharply to her mother who gave her a reassuring hug.
>
> Then the lady asked if they'd like to have another go, and gave the teddy a different card to read. '*I got left on a heater but I'm okay now. Please don't stare at me.*' This was less hostile, and Amy began to relax and smile, perhaps at the bear's gruff voice.
>
> The bear had a third card so they decided to get the bear to read out that one too. '*I got left on a heater but I'm okay now. That's a strange blue picture there on the wall. What do you think it is?*' Amy told the bear it was a picture of birds flying – and the bear's strange fur passed from our attention.

Showing and teaching – *Having something to say*

Having something to say should be part of helping a new pupil, or a pupil who is returning after an illness or injury has changed the way they look, to settle in at school (see p. 33). When familiarity has been achieved within school, the issue of surprise, curiosity and unwanted attention may arise only infrequently and quite unexpectedly. (Encountering visitors to the school or during a trip out, for instance.) These occasions are vital learning opportunities for children and young people who are visibly different.

Children learn much by seeing and experiencing what other people do, especially the adults around them. Staff need to be alert and well-prepared. As above, the most effective responses have three components:

1   Recognize that it is *normal* to react with curiosity and concern upon first encountering someone with a disfigurement. 'You've noticed Callum's unusual hands.'
2   Respond 'easily' with just enough information and reassurance to enable the other person to settle their thoughts. 'He has a condition called Apert's.'
3   Change the subject or move the attention on. 'Callum and the others in his class have been creating this frieze along the corridor.'

In this way Callum learns that people do notice, that a little information helps, and that it is possible to take control of a potentially awkward situation rather than falling prey to it. When he is ready, he will be able to speak up for himself. 'Don't mind my hands – it's just Apert's. Look, we're making butterflies by folding the paper.'

Deciding what to say

Small children seem to get on best with just one simple sentence. Older children and teenagers need to develop a range of options for different kinds of encounters.

If a child already has words that they are comfortable with, for example 'It's my birthmark', this should form the basis for the explanation which is used – 'It's Kylie's birthmark.' If not, school staff, parents and child will need to work sensitively together to arrive at something which feels comfortable and right. Acting out little scenes to see how different words and phrases feel can be useful.

A child who is interested in written letters and words, or is beginning to read, might like to have each option in turn, for a day or two, on a small piece of coloured card, to carry in their pocket or put by their bed. This can help them to prefer or reject words and phrases which may all seem equally strange at first.

> *It's just the way my head is.*
> *The bone on this side doesn't grow so fast.*
> *The doctor's got a long name for it but I can't remember it.*
> *It's called hemifacial microsomia.*
> *It's just how I was born.*

It will be best for the child if everyone uses the same form of explanation, both in and out of school. It is important, also, to check from time to time how the child feels about their phrase or sentence.

Case study

Jake, whose legs were mildly affected by cerebral palsy, was wondering how to tell his new classmates about the problem he would sometimes have keeping up with them. At the core of his worries was the risk that mentioning cerebral palsy would soon lead someone to use 'the S-word' – which he could not contemplate. He briefed Eddie, a good friend from primary school who was going with him to the same secondary school, to give a very short talk to his new class on the first day of term. Eddie explained what caused cerebral palsy, that Jake's legs were slightly affected, and asked everyone to be careful in doorways and on stairs. Jake subsequently reported with great relief that he had not heard anyone use the S-word.

An accident?

As it happens, using the word 'accident' can trigger rather than resolve curiosity and discussion. *Accident? How did it happen? Whose fault was it?* A short phrase about what actually happened is more effective. 'Kanu's face and hands were burned in a fire.' 'Emma was bitten by a dog.' 'Jack was in a house-fire.' 'The car Martin was in crashed and caught fire.' 'Issy fell through a glass door.'

Useful phrases for managing unwanted attention

I got burned in a fire. It doesn't bother me. Don't let it bother you.

It's just how I was born. It affects my face and hands but . . .

Don't mind my skin – it's just eczema gone crazy. You can't catch it but the itching drives me mad. It really helps to change the subject . . .

I put my face on inside out this morning, ok? You'll get used to it.

It's just a skin thing. You can't catch it.

I put my face on inside out this morning, okay? You'll get used to it.

It's just the way my face is. It makes me easy to spot in photos.

You think my nose is weird? You should see my teeth! (*B-I-G smile*)

It's scars from a fire. It was bad at the time but I'm okay now. *Then change the subject* . . . 'You wanna play football?'

It's called a cleft. Imagine a kind of gap in the top of your mouth. They do operations to gradually fix it. Have you heard the joke about a maths teacher who couldn't do sums?

It's just something I was born with. It's got some complicated name and people notice my bumps a lot at first but then you just get used to how I look and really I'm just a regular guy.

I got burned in a fire. Please don't stare.

I got bad cuts when I fell through a glass door. I had to go to hospital. Have you ever been in hospital?

I know I look a bit different, but it's cool to be different. Tell me something different about you.

You seem to think my hands are interesting. It's just a condition called Apert's. Tell me something interesting about you.

It's just the way I was born. Everybody's different and some people are more different than others, but please don't stare.

Children need an all-purpose response or a range of responses for different kinds of situations. They also need an option which, without being rude, makes it clear that they don't like excessive attention being given to the way they look.

All these responses to staring or up-front questions are best followed by changing the subject in an ordinary, sociable way. However, if the child is asserting their desire not to be looked at, they then need to walk away, get on with their work or their lunch, or otherwise break the contact, after they have spoken.

Older children and young people can benefit from more explicit training in *Having something to say*. With a group of friends, for example, they can envisage scenarios and develop suitable phrases and sentences. It takes practice and courage to 'go live' – but the rewards are being more in control and more socially effective.

'I just want them not to stare. Saying something – it just isn't the point. Rude people don't deserve an explanation.'

Parents and children do have tough experiences with rude and intrusive strangers (see a parent's account of a supermarket incident on p. 16). These unpleasant incidents need to be acknowledged. The process of accepting – but *in no way condoning* – that this is what some people do, is an essential part of modelling *Having something to say*.

It was at a pantomime and this other family didn't want to sit near us – because of my eczema is the point here. Their Mum – not the kids actually – she was making all this fuss. My Mum turned her back on them and gave us all this 'look' that says '*Oh! This is so not necessary.*' Sort of part-bored, part-amazed. It makes you feel, we're fine, it's these other people that the men in white coats are coming for.

There is clearly a crucial distinction to be made between a new person's initial 'unsure' reaction and unreasonable, persistent or intrusive staring, questioning, comments or other hostile reactions. While some awkwardness and curiosity from others is 'normal' and is best dealt with by *Having something to say,* children and young people must also be supported when someone's reaction goes beyond this. Strategies for this are described in Chapter 5.

'It's all right here. Every one knows everyone.'

There are small rural communities and neighbourhood schools serving a network of local streets where families all know each other and 'outsiders' are rarely encountered.

> When it really hit me was when we went on holiday to this place that specialised in activities for children . . . Right from our first break at a motorway service area – every minute there was someone else having a good gawp at our Jodi. It really got to me. The whole week, all these strangers whispering to each other behind their hands. I couldn't wait to get home. I just wanted someone to say 'Hi, Jodi,' like they all do around here, instead of staring.

Being accepted by her friendly local community will give Jodi every chance of developing good social skills and a positive, sociable outlook. But she will also need to learn some specialized strategies for coping with the new people she encounters when she moves beyond her familiar neighbourhood.

When a child's speech is affected

Having something to say uses a spoken message to counter 'unsure' reactions to unusual appearance. For children and young people whose disfiguring injury or condition affects their speech (and for children whose speech is 'different' but not their appearance) speaking may risk increasing rather than decreasing the other person's 'unsure' reaction. Other people rarely if ever listen much to people who speak differently (except when abroad). It can take time to become familiar with the sounds and begin to grasp the meaning being conveyed. A child may be ridiculed by others for their unusual-sounding speech (although classmates can also be very good at 'interpreting' for an unfamiliar teacher, for instance.) It can be particularly difficult to convey the desired 'inner self' quality (see pp. 82–3) if the other person confuses, as many people do, impaired speech with impaired thinking.

However, children with substantial expressive language difficulties are motivated to communicate, even though it is a frustrating experience.[9] Managing staring when out and about, and achieving good 'ephemeral interactions' and first encounters with new people are crucial for self-esteem,[10] and maintaining the motivation to communicate,[11] as well as being important life skills for young people and adults who are visibly different.

School staff should model *Having something to say* (see p. 22) regardless of their expectations of the child's eventual ability to speak up for themselves. They should also seek long-term collaboration with their pupil's speech and language therapist (part of their specialist medical team for pupils with clefts and other cranio-facial conditions). The involvement of parents or carers is very important too.

A number of aspects and options (which can usefully be combined) may need to be explored, to see how the child or young person can maximize their ability to cope effectively with brief and ephemeral encounters when out and about, and to have effective first encounters when meeting new people. (This may be quite different from and additional to other therapeutic work being undertaken to develop the pupil's speaking and language abilities.)

Non-verbal communication

'Eye contact is a basic requirement for successful interaction. Pupils with speech and language difficulties often learn to look away and not to make eye contact with the person who is speaking or listening to them. This is likely to be interpreted negatively by adults.'[12] Through good eye-contact and body language, and effective use of gesture, a child or young person can do much to get the other person on their side.

Non-verbal version	Hoped-for meaning received by the other person
Eye-contact, smile if possible, followed by a small gesture with the head and hands (like a conductor getting an orchestra to pause and pay attention).	Be reassured and please pay attention. I'm about to say something that you'll have a struggle to understand.
After speaking – eye-contact, questioning look on brow, questioning gesture with shoulders and offering gesture with hands	Did you get that? Do you need me to have another go?
Eye-contact, offering gesture with hands – one hand 'writing' on palm of other hand.	Would it help if I wrote it down?

Flashcards

One boy showed new people a small card:

> *I can talk but it might be hard to understand.*
> *Are you up for that?*

to find out whether he had any kind of a chance with the other person.

   Another used the text facility on his mobile (no need to send, just show the other person) to 'get through':

FACE-SPEECH-UNUSUAL.
LETS DO IT LIKE THIS TO
START WITH.

Synthesized speech

This has been established as completely 'cool' by Professor Stephen Hawking, who has even appeared, using his synthesized voice, on *The Simpsons*. For pupils whose speech is most severely affected, this equipment may be available. In this case the pupil may like to create two or three pre-set statements for use with new people, and see how they get on:

Hello. I'm Michael. Please excuse this gadget. What's your name?

In the fullness of time, a smaller, simpler, less specialized and less expensive device will probably become available – somewhere between a Gameboy and a Palm or PDA – which includes a voice facility. It is possible to envisage a child or young person using this with some style when out and about, and when getting started with new people.

Pupils who use other forms of communication – symbols, pictures, signing, total communication – will rarely if ever encounter anyone beyond close family, peers and staff linked to special educational needs in school, and the speech and language people they meet in hospital, who is familiar with their method of communicating. It could be argued, therefore, that the goal of inclusion requires everyone to learn something about alternative or augmentative communication systems. Meanwhile, it may be that good self-talk and associated body language (see p. 51) and the presence of someone to interpret will be required. (Teenagers, however, do no like depending on adults when 'hanging out'.[13])

'We haven't said anything to him yet. We're waiting until he's ready – until he asks.'

The drawback with delaying is that the child will already be at least vaguely aware that other people sometimes look at him or her in a certain way – perhaps in a way that seems to bother mummy and daddy. The child may not have said anything because he or she has picked up that his parents don't want him to – that *they* aren't ready. For more about the pros and cons of waiting until a small child 'is ready', see p. 32.

Considering siblings

If a facially disfigured pupil has a brother or sister, *Having something to say* will be useful for them too, as they may well be asked about their sibling's difference. This is easier to do if they are at the same school. If not, it requires liaison with the relevant teacher at their own school. Having a simple answer at the ready can build confidence and protect against hassle from peers who know (and their teachers may not know) that there is a child at home or at another school who is 'different'.

For all of us

When, on the bus, a small child notices a stranger with an unusual face (or a limping pigeon with a missing foot) we ourselves need to have prepared and rehearsed *having something to say*.

To prepare your own answers, take a careful look in the mirror so that you can talk easily about exactly what you look like:

'Hey! Look at that man! What's the matter with his nose?'
'I guess that's just the way his nose is. Mine's pink with orange freckles. What's your nose like?'

When the little girl was staring at the pigeon, what could her mother have said instead of turning away to study the departures board? Almost anything would do – except 'Don't stare' – and its corollary, turning away. For example:

'That pigeon manages very well, don't you think, with just the one foot? She looks as if she just ignores it and gets on with being a busy pigeon.'

All of us need to be alert to opportunities to be ordinary, straightforward and positive about all our differences.

Chapter 3

A new pupil or a pupil returning from hospital

Looking different

For children who 'look different' each new start, from playgroup to college and beyond, means encountering all those initial reactions all over again – staring, avoiding, furtive glances, surprise, interest, embarrassment, concern. From playschool to college, there are many transitions – each new start is an opportunity to practise encountering new people positively and effectively.

When events alter a child's or young person's appearance there is usually a period of absence from school: weeks or months, while they recover from serious burns, a couple of weeks following planned surgery, or a day or two once or twice a term for periodic laser treatment of a birthmark. When the pupil returns to school, careful preparations and appropriate interventions can help them learn how to manage other people's reactions – now and in future new situations too.

Talking with parents...

When their baby was born looking 'different', or when their child became disfigured by an injury or illness or the onset of a condition, the parent(s) may have had good, informed support, or they may have coped largely alone as best they could. It is useful for the school to ask whether the parent has support if and when they feel the need. If the parent asks for help, or if it is not clear who else is going to make an appropriate referral, it may be appropriate for the school to help set this up:

- Is there a support group locally? nationally? Do they mainly provide information? Are they busy fund-raising to help scientists 'find a cure'? Do they focus on children's needs (or on 'fun' for the children), or is there real support there for parents too?
- What can health and social services offer locally? How do they take referrals? What are their criteria for offering help? How long is the waiting list?
- If a referral is made it is useful to ask, periodically, how they're getting on (taking care not let this question give the impression that they don't seem to be managing).

Note that this is different from the local education authority providing a support worker, link person or advocate to help parents during the assessment of and provision for their child's special educational needs.

...about your pre-school, school or college

Ethos is very important, and may have been a factor in the choice of playgroup, school or college. Parents may be articulate and well-prepared, which can be useful, or rather intimidating. Parents who are more easy-going or less articulate may appear to be less concerned about their child's welfare – but, as usual, appearances can deceive.

It can be useful to address parents' key concerns whether or not they are explicit:

- How do you enable each individual child to feel equally important and that they fully belong, when they all have such different abilities, learning styles and needs, wide-ranging family backgrounds and previous experiences of being with other children?
- What do you know about disfigurement in general and this child's disfiguring injury or condition in particular? What can you do to address this child's particular needs?
- If a child finds it difficult to join in, because they are shy and quiet, or because their language or cognitive development is delayed, or because other children don't seem to take to them, what can you do to help?
- What approach do you take when difficulties such as teasing or bullying arise between children, in the playground for instance?
- What about special educational needs and/or periodic or ongoing medical or treatment needs? What if hospital visits may interrupt future school attendance?
- For people of all ages who are visibly different, out in the ordinary 'able-bodied' world, how do you see the issues? Is it about supporting them to learn and adapt to the demands of society at large? Or do you think in terms of everyone (including schools) making changes so that everyone can be more fully included?

...about their child and his or her needs and potentialities

Educational concerns often focus on enabling pupils to access the curriculum. Parents may be strongly concerned for their child to be accepted and to mix well with their peers. They may be 'over-protective' as they struggle with all the unwanted attention associated with their child's appearance. They may talk in a medicalized way about the injury, illness or condition that has affected their child, or in a way which makes their child 'special'. If their child has other special needs associated with the injury or condition that affects the way they look, they may have additional concerns about how these will be met at school. They may only want their child 'to be treated like everyone else'.

School staff must map out a path which visits but does not get lost in the various hinterlands of disfigurement – special, included, individual, one-of-the-crowd, educational achievement, social development.

'We haven't said anything to him yet. We're waiting until he asks.'

Parents may have sheltered their child from other people's staring, nervousness, concern, etc. by avoiding public situations. 'It' may never have been talked about (within the child's hearing). A very small child may *seem* unaware of their difference. There is some evidence that younger children make fewer judgements regarding facial difference[1] but none that they don't notice.[2]

A decision 'not to mention it (yet)' risks:

- undermining the child's sense of reality, which is that other people do notice them and stare or look away
- complicating the child's process of developing the skills and confidence which they will need long-term to deal with other people's reactions
- teaching the child that these things cannot or must not be talked about
- promoting the pretence or the ideal that we are all the same when, clearly, we are not
- endorsing the disempowering *wish* that people would not react or behave as they do
- modelling anxiety, defensiveness or annoyance in social situations because of having no effective response prepared for people's (adults' as well as children's) curiosity or comments
- giving the confusing message to other children who may be present that sometimes we don't say a word about staring and curiosity, although they have been told on other occasions not to stare.

If, after suitably sensitive and concerned discussions about meeting their child's and the other children's needs, a parent still prefers that their child's difference is not to be mentioned, this must be respected.[3] For the other children, whose curiosity will be real enough, a solution can take the form – 'When anyone asks we give the answer, "It's just the way she is."'

Information

Case study

Ahmed, 5, had one ordinary arm. The other arm stopped, with no hand, at his elbow. His prosthetic arm hung at his side, unused. The occupational therapist (OT) observed, in sessions with Ahmed, that without the prosthetic arm in place, he used his 'short arm' for things like holding paper steady when he was writing. It was agreed that he should have more choice about whether or not to wear his prosthetic arm at school.

Staff noticed that several children became noisy around Ahmed at playtimes. One girl refused to sit next to him and became distressed when the teacher tried to insist. The next day, the girl's mother complained: Layla had not slept all night, terrified of the dragon who came and bit off the arms of sleeping children who'd been naughty. She hadn't sat next to Ahmed and that was naughty so she dare not go to sleep.

Another of Ahmed's classmates finally explained that when Ahmed's arm had suddenly disappeared, that's what she'd thought must have happened.

'We had a gentle talk with Ahmed's parents. They'd never known what to tell their son about his arm and were obviously troubled by this. In the end the OT took advice and suggested referring to it as his 'short arm' and explaining that it was just the way he was born. We all went with that and did some other activities with the children about all being different and all having things in common. What we've learnt is that if you don't have answers ready, the children will devise their own.'

Information helps settle other people's curiosity and concern, but it is also important to respect the ordinary privacy which is accorded to families and individuals in general. Parents need their children's teachers to be clear what information about their child is *for*.

- Certain key staff need in-depth information to ensure the child's education goes well both academically and socially, and potential difficulties can be anticipated and adequately addressed.
- More basic information is needed by other staff involved regularly or occasionally, so that learning experiences can be positive and appropriate – as with any pupil.
- Brief, basic 'answers' are needed by *all* staff in order to manage other children's (and their own) reactions effectively (see p. 23).

Bringing everyone on board

Staff

In order to feel informed and effective in their work, staff can benefit from the following options:

1   An information session.
2   In-service training including more background about the social psychology of appearance and disfigurement – 'counter-intuitive' research findings show how it can be hard, otherwise, to get things right for themselves and their pupils.
3   An information sheet giving clear guidance on how to respond to staring and questions that they may encounter (see Olivia's case study and Amy Darling's information sheets).

All staff need to feel informed and comfortable in their work with pupils who are visibly different – support staff, language assistants, canteen staff and lunchtime supervisors, administrative staff, parents and any other volunteers who come in to help, supply staff and other visiting professionals, and school governors.

Case study

Olivia had an extensive strawberry birthmark. At home she got on well with her brothers and sisters. But her parents could see that, when it came to starting nursery school, there would be concern and questions. As her birthmark prevented Olivia from speaking, they created an information sheet to answer all the questions other people might want to ask her (see Olivia's information sheet, 'Some information about Olivia (Livvy)').

Everyone at the nursery had a copy and whenever someone had a worry or a question, there was someone with an answer nearby. Copies went home to parents too: if a classmate took their questions home, their parent(s) would be able to provide just the answer and reassurance required.

Olivia got on very well at her nursery and an updated information sheet was used when she moved to infant school. Her older brother, already a pupil at the school, learned to answer sensible questions about his sister, and to say, 'I've answered enough questions for now' when he got fed up with it all.

SOME INFORMATION ABOUT OLIVIA (LIVVY)

What is that Red lumpy mark on her face?

It is commonly known as a strawberry but it is in fact a mixed capillary and cavernous haemangioma. A haemangioma is a malformation of blood vessels.

Is it catching?

No.

Does it hurt her?

No, but it does get hotter than the rest of her body and sometimes it gets itchy. If it gets scratched it bleeds more easily than the rest of her body.

Can she see out of that eye?

Yes.

What is that tube in her neck?

It is called a tracheostomy tube. and Livvy needs to keep this tube in all the time to help her to breathe.

Why?

She has a rare complication where a strawberry haemangioma has grown inside her throat blocking off most of her airway.

What it that machine that Livvy has with her?

It is a suction machine- Sometimes mucous forms in the tracheostomy tube that Livvy cannot cough up and this machine sucks it out. It's like a mechanical way of blowing you nose.

Why doesn't Livvy talk?

You need lots of breath coming out of your mouth to talk, and most of Livvys breath comes out of her tube instead and so there's not enough left to talk with.

How much does Livvy hear and understand?

Livvy hears everything and probably understands almost as much as any other 2 1/2 year old. By a mixture of signs, gestures and body language. She doesn't use a standard sign language.

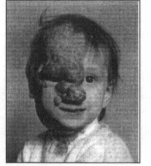

What is the tube in Livvys tummy for?

Livvy finds it difficult to swallow because of the haemangioma in her throat, so she is fed mainly through the tube in her tummy with a special liquid feed. She can drink water and eat very smooth food.

Why has Livvy got all of these problems?

We don't know, Complications with strawberry haemangiomas are rare, but small strawberry marks are quite common (about 3 in every 100 babies born will have a type of haemangioma - a salmon patch, strawberry mark or port wine stain). Strawberry marks are more common in girls than boys and no one knows why the occur.

Will Livvy ever get better?

Yes, every year the strawberry fades on her face and it is shrinking in her throat. By the time she goes to school her tubes should be out and her face a lot better. She will however still need major plastic surgery at some stage.

An extra note from Livvy's Parents

In spite of Livvys appearance, medical conditions and tubes she is a normal, lively little girl. Her face is not a problem to her, us or other people that know and love her, so please don't let it be a problem for you. The world is full of different people and children are very accepting if pointed in the right direction by adults. Questions and worries should be answered honestly and anything you don't know then please feel free to ask Sally or us.

Figure 3.1 Olivia's information sheet (see case study)

New pupil Amy Darling – notes for staff

Amy will be joining us in September. She has an unusual appearance due to a condition called 'Goldenhar'. One side of her face is smaller than the other and the ear is also affected. Amy deals with her partial hearing loss very sensibly. Next year she will undergo a prolonged surgical process to improve this asymmetry. Meanwhile, Amy's appearance is very noticeably 'different' – you will no doubt find yourself taking an extra-long look when you first see Amy, and so will everyone else.

Please use the following notes to guide your response to pupils who stare or ask about Amy. Amy is not yet quite ready to deal with curiosity from people she does not know, but she does talk about it sometimes with people she has got to know – though she says it really isn't interesting compared with the other things friends talk about.

You see a pupil staring at Amy	*A pupil ask you about Amy's unusual appearance*
'You seem to have zoomed in on Amy's unusual face. It's called Goldenhar – some of the bone in your face doesn't grow so much. It doesn't bother her, don't let it bother you.'	'It's called Goldenhar. If you have Goldenhar the various parts of your face don't all grow in quite the usual way. It doesn't bother Amy – don't let it bother you.'
Then either: 'You could try saying Hi and introducing yourself since she's/ you're both new to the school.' *or:* 'You're just in time' (then make a suitable positive change of subject, e.g. 'to help me carry this gear back to the gym')	*Then either:* Suggest a sociable gesture *or . . .* Move the subject onto something else that's natural and appropriate, such as 'Have you got a bus to catch?'

If a pupil still seems preoccupied, please arrange for them to see Mr Cage, head of Year 7, before afternoon registration the next day.

Keep this info sheet in your diary. Thank you all. Have a lovely summer.

John Cage

Pupils or students

> if encouraged by adults, non-handicapped . . . children will increase levels of inter-action with handicapped children [and] have been observed, for example, to adapt their communication to the appropriate cognitive 'level' of their peers . . . [A]daptive communications and relatively frequent social interactions . . . help lessen the risk status of handicapped children.[4]

Clearly it is important to encourage children to interact across barriers of difference. But how is this best done?

Should we give a talk?

A health professional from the pupil's specialist clinic or burns unit may offer to give the children 'a talk' about the injury or condition that affects the child. The child's parent may suggest this or offer to do it themselves. It can seem useful to share information with the children. But does it promote inclusive attitudes and behaviour?

Carefully and imaginatively devised information and play sessions were run[5] to inform a group of hearing children about the deafness of some other children who were to join the class. But after the hearing children had learnt about deafness, they showed *fewer* social initiations towards their deaf peers than the 'uninformed' control group.

Similar unexpected difficulties following other information sessions (talks, assemblies, etc.) have led to more thoughts about the possible reasons for the weakness of this approach to inclusion. Why might this be?

- Talking about a child makes them 'special' or 'different'. The others, sitting listen-ing, are then ordinary or all the same, their individuality on hold.
- The other children's curiosity is satisfied so there is less motivation to get talking to the 'different' classmate.
- Talking about the injury, illness or condition that affects the way a child looks misses the point because the staring and curiosity are the barrier.
- It makes the child being talked about seem alien. (The word 'Martians' can be sub-stituted very nicely for 'deaf children' throughout the Vandell account reported above.)
- It does not resemble in any way the usual process of getting to know someone new.
- From the other children's perspective, it substitutes talking with him or her your-selves with listening to someone talking about this child. 'Like . . . they don't want you to do that?'
- It's suddenly very formal and important and the grown-ups are in charge of everything. It's *their* stuff.
- The children don't take it all in – their minds wander. Then when they see the child who was talked about, they realize there's something they've been told and they're not sure if they remember what. 'Suppose I get it wrong?'

Until we know more about this it seems better to share information with children and young people about a new or newly different classmate, more interactively and conversa-tionally – by responding to natural curiosity with straightforward answers (see pp. 22 and 34–5).

There is some anecdotal evidence that if a pupil talks about themselves to a group of peers, the results can be positive – see 'Tom's assembly', p. 86. Also, 'a talk' can have a positive effect when the focus is on how newcomers might best be made to feel welcome:

> Head or class teacher asks, 'What do friendly children say to a new pupil out in the playground?'
>
> Pupils' suggestions soon flow: 'Hello, my name's Sonny, what's your name?' 'I've got a new puppy. Have you got any pets?' 'Would you like to play football with us?' 'Would you like to sit on our table at lunchtime?' 'Some of us are going swimming on Saturday – would you like to come along?'

Other ways to promote inclusive attitudes and behaviour are described in Chapter 4.

How are they doing?

Even if the pupil has a Statement of Special Educational Needs with an annual review, something less formal but more frequent is advisable.

Review checklist

- *During breaks and lunchtimes*
  Frequency and quality of interactions with peers? – with adults?
  Does this pupil have the (social) skills they need to join in games?
  If they try and fail to join in – what exactly happens?
- *More generally at school and in home neighbourhood*
  Does this pupil make and keep friends?
  How well do they 'read' other people's feelings and reactions?
  How well do they express their own feelings and reactions?
- *Encountering people they haven't met before*
  How often does this pupil experience new people or new situations?
  How do they deal with other people's responses to their unusual appearance?
- *Communication*
  Do they have the language they need to talk about their experiences (and worries) – which may include events or feelings which are not shared by anyone else they know?
- *Ask the pupil him- or herself*
  Do they enjoy breaks and lunchtimes or are they glad when the bell goes?
  Do they have friends?
  Are there situations at school when they don't feel relaxed and comfortable? When? What? How could this be improved?
  How do they get on when there's someone new around who hasn't met them before?
  Are they able to go places and do things they want to do? Or are they held back by worries about being stared at or asked questions or feeling conspicuous?
  For older children and young people: what ideas do they have for their future?

- *Lessons, homework, tasks, learning*

  Educational progress needs to be carefully monitored as pupils with disfigurements may have both their strengths and any areas of difficulty overlooked by their teachers.[6] (Teachers may be reluctant to observe a child closely who has a disfigurement, in case this is uncomfortable for them – or for the teacher.)

  How aware is this pupil of their abilities at school? Do they know when it might be useful to ask for help, and have they the confidence to ask? Are there any areas of particular difficulty (possibly unconnected with their disfigurement) and/or any marked talents or aptitudes?

Moving on

It was about day three when Toby came home and asked me, Mummy what's *ugly*?' I think that's the hardest question I've had to answer so far.

Toni and Holly and me, we used to always go swimming and we still did at first. I used to phone and we'd meet up at the pool like we used to. Then it was gradually sort of dawning on me that it was always me that phoned and often they said they had too much homework and stuff. Then it was the Christmas holidays and my cousin was over from Ireland and we went swimming and there they were – Toni and Holly and a couple of other girls in our year at the new school. I kind of tried to shrug it off but later Katie my cousin said she could see I was gutted. She worked really hard keeping me occupied and having fun at the other side of the pool. I would like to ask Holly or Toni about it, just to know if I'm being paranoid or if they really did decide to leave me out and if so why. My hunch is that when they said 'Let's phone Alli', those other two, the new girls, said '*Oh no not her!*' Without even bothering to get to know me, like all I am is the one with the weird birthmark. Which would mean that Toni and Holly didn't stick up for me, even though we were friends all through primary. That is so not okay.

Case study

Ella had mild learning difficulties and a disfiguring condition affecting her face. When she transferred to secondary school her family and school staff were concerned as to how she would cope socially. Information sessions were arranged for staff about the social issues associated with disfigurement and about the specific condition which affected Ella's appearance and the associated learning difficulties.

During subsequent follow-up enquiries, Ella was described as a confident and sociable girl who enjoyed school and was well accepted by all her classmates. She was also described as being happy at home in her village.

After Christmas in her last year at school, a new request for help was initiated by the careers adviser. Ella was not sufficiently academically able for any of the courses available in the sixth form at her school. But she would not visit college to see what college was like. (The careers adviser later commented that Ella had told her she would never have children because she wouldn't want them to go through what she had been through. This appeared to be the only indication that Ella sometimes had a very hard time.)

The annual review was brought forward. During this meeting it emerged that, although she had several friends of her own age at school, Ella never went out without her mother or older sister. Her work experience placement had been at a small nursery for children with severe learning difficulties – arranged at the last minute because the owner of a local kennels where she had arranged to go had pulled out, saying her appearance would distress customers.[7] Ella now felt that she would never be accepted anywhere except among severely handicapped people and their helpers.

Ella's Statement of Special Educational Needs addressed her cognitive difficulties, which had been met throughout her secondary education. It was acknowledged that more should have been done to ensure Ella was better prepared socially for life after school.

The option of an additional year at school was created: among other project work, much of it necessarily individual, the programme included errands and trips, work experience and college visits, to help Ella learn and practise social skills for dealing effectively with other people's reactions to her appearance.

The more 'no-one notices any more' in the child's current establishment, the bigger the risk when the time comes to move (see Ella's case study). Older children are more judgemental.[8] Children who have disfigurements tend to have a smaller network of friends.[9] Teenagers, anxious about their own appearance, can become intolerant of difference. For a child or young person with a facial disfigurement, moving on can feel like being thrown to the lions.

Without time and support to learn and practise strategies for dealing with staring, meeting new people, and developing extra social skills, all the good work done in one playgroup or school may be 'lost' during the transition to the new school or college.

Secondary school was big but after a while I seemed to have seen and been seen by pretty well everyone there. And got to know a good few of them. Here [at college] the numbers are vast – an endless supply of staring and turning away and pointing me out to whoever they're with. There are college rules about smoking and mobile phones, but there isn't one about saying hello. Unfortunately.

Transition checklist

1 Be assured that this is a specialized area: children and young people are extremely vulnerable in new situations. Research into the social and psychological aspects of difference show that well-intentioned 'common sense' approaches may not be helpful.

2 Identify a single, named member of staff at the new establishment with responsibility for ensuring that everything is done to facilitate a successful transition. They need to be in regular contact with the named member of staff at the pupil's current school.

3 Either this person or another named member of staff needs to be available as someone the new pupil or student can go to for help or advice if anything goes wrong.

4 Promote positive and inclusive attitudes and behaviour by requiring all teaching staff to run at least one substantial and relevant learning activity involving all the pupils or students they teach, drawn and adapted from those outlined in Chapter 4 (i.e. not focusing on a pupil or student's 'difference').

5 Establish good, open and interested professional relations with the parent(s) and the young person whose appearance is 'different'.

6 Involve them in considering how unfamiliar people may react before they have got to know them. Does the new pupil or student have effective strategies for dealing with curiosity, staring, comments, etc.? Do they need help (and time) to develop and practise this?

7 If there are any siblings already at the new school or college, check whether they are equipped as at (6).

8 If friends and acquaintances are transferring with this young person, check whether they are equipped as at (6).

9 Consider carefully what information needs to be shared with whom. See *Information* pp. 32–3 above.

10 The staff member named at (3) needs to seek out the new pupil or student and ask them how things are going. If they say 'okay' ask more questions – use the *review checklist* on pp. 37–8 above. If any difficulties emerge, identify tasks and people to resolve or improve things, and arrange a follow-up meeting to monitor progress.

11 With the child or young person, monitor and record the whole process – each transition is both a vital step which needs to go well for them, and an opportunity to rehearse, review and improve their approach to all new ventures that they will undertake in future.

12 Repeat 10 and 11 until all is well.

I had this idea for a big coloured badge saying, *It's called Nf. You can ask me about it if you like.* What do you think? And I'm practising asking questions too, as well as having something to say.

Chapter 4

Creating inclusive school communities

> Attendance at a mainstream school, whilst seen by the majority of disabled young people to be preferable, did not necessarily make things any easier in that it produced a different experience of isolation. Many of the [visibly different] young people attending local mainstream schools found that they were constantly being 'left out', made to feel different, socially isolated and sometimes physically bullied.[1]

Looking different makes a pupil vulnerable to isolation. The school is located within a social world already shaped by other rules and norms, other priorities, other styles of interaction.

Don't stare is a rule which most people internalize in childhood. Pp. 1–2 in the *Introduction* gives more on the consequences of '*Don't stare*'. Chapters 2 and 7 set out skills and strategies which a child or young person who looks different can use to help reverse this. However, for a social environment to be inclusive, everyone needs to know how to greet and acknowledge everyone else, regardless of appearance and difference.

The importance of friendship is emphasized in much that is written about child development and education. However, having no friends is not unusual or uncommon.[2] 'In any given sociometric study 10% of the children were not selected as a friend by any other child.'[3] 'Among adolescents . . . 20% reported having no friends'.[4] Children who look different are more likely to have fewer friends, and may have none, but they are not alone – for a significant minority of people, both children and adults, having friends is not a part of their day-to-day lives. For school structures and arrangements to be fully inclusive, they must support the 'loner' (who may or may not be lonely[5]) as well as pupils who hang out together.

Goodness and beauty are prevalent throughout our media, providing images where the dominant message – often the only message – is concerned with appearance, style, fashion, perfection. (a) For anyone who looks different, this poses a considerable challenge. What are they themselves to make of looking the way they do? How are they to get others to see them as the people they are rather than in terms of their disfigured appearance – as tragic, or heroic, or weird? (b) For everyone, this both makes appearance an overriding concern and narrows the field of 'okayness' – skin not right, hair not right, teeth not right, body-shape not right . . . For school to be inclusive, images are needed which counter this media bias – images of difference and images of other qualities as well as appearance.

The curriculum, and the teaching and learning through which children and young people access it, is a key area for action. All staff must find opportunities to promote inclusion. An example is given here of how a school subject – mathematics – which may not be the most likely candidate for promoting inclusive (or non-inclusive) attitudes and behaviour, can engage pupils in the cause of both excellence and inclusion (see pp. 46–7).

Greeting and acknowledging each other – making the social environment inclusive

A few weeks after changing schools due to serious bullying, a Year 7 pupil with a distinctive face commented:

> It's much nicer here. At [the previous school] it was like you had to press yourself flat against the corridor walls because anyone coming the other way might give you a shove or say something. Here you can just walk where you're going without trying to hide.
>
> Before I moved, at school people were always saying things like, 'How's it going, One-eye?' Or they'd walk by as if you weren't there at all – which isn't nice but it's better than clever-dick stuff. When I started here, at first I thought they were taking the micky – you know, saying hello, standing back to let you go first through the door – I'd be on guard for some sort of trick or like they were patronizing me. But everyone here really does nod or smile and say hello. One time I was in the dinner hall and someone sat down opposite me and said, you know, some in-your-face comment. The girl sitting next to me, who wasn't even in my year, turned to me and said, 'Some people have very bad manners.' She said it to me, and I did appreciate it, but she said it loud enough for the rude girl opposite to hear too, and I appreciated that so much.

A year after starting work, a new teacher recalled:

> I was dismayed at first at what I took to be the children's rudeness – not acknowledging your presence, not saying hello, not smiling. As if I was invisible or they wished I was. What I didn't want to do was go along with this – as if it's all right to just ignore each other. But I had no particular idea about *doing* anything to improve things. Then one morning when I passed a lad in my form lounging on the steps, I said, 'Good morning Brendon,' as is my wont, and when he blanked me as usual, I replied on his behalf, 'Hello Mrs Deal,' and gave him a smile. Well, why not? Next time I said 'Hello Brendon,' on some staircase or other, he astonished me by replying, 'Hello Mrs Deal,' with a smile. It's beginning to catch on – maybe I'm known as the teacher you have to say hello to or she'll embarrass you. Or did they just not know about greetings?

School rules:

1   On corridors, stairs, in doorways, etc. when you pass someone you don't know, nod or smile and say hello.
2   When you see someone you do know, nod or smile and say hello.
3   When you see someone whose unusual appearance tends to make you stare or look more or look away, nod or smile and say hello.

For pupils who are 'loners' as well as those with friends

during the early years of childhood, solitary or non-social activity is actually quite normal [so] . . . there is little reason for non-social players to be singled out *by their peers* as [deviating from] age-group play norms . . . [Increased] sociability and . . . decline in solitary activity with age may account for the finding that during the mid- and late years of childhood, children who are socially withdrawn become increasingly salient to their age-mates. . . . Their deviation from age-appropriate social norms may well result in the establishment of negative peer reputations. Indeed, by . . . mid- to late . . . childhood, social withdrawal and anxiety are as strongly correlated with peer rejection and unpopularity as is aggression.[6]

[As] children begin to be aware of themselves as social beings . . . acute self-consciouss shyness [has been observed in] some children. Labelled 'late developing shyness' by Buss (1986), this acute self-consciousness may be caused by a lack of or too much attention from others. In the case of children with craniofacial deformities, a feeling of conspicuousness may result [from] the realization of the differences between self and others. The experiences of being stared at . . . increase the likelihood of children withdrawing from social situations.[7]

Do these people feel badly about this? Do they wish they had friends? Or do they prefer to be alone? Sociable people who enjoy doing things in groups cannot but think that they must be lonely – or *strange*. There is not, in fact, a strong link between lack of friends and feeling lonely.[8] However, people without friends have certain needs which, for others, are addressed by the having of friends.

Safety and protection – exploring new places[9]

Particularly at transition from infant to junior school or from primary to secondary school, how can exploring a new environment be facilitated so that all new pupils get the chance to become fully orientated and self-assured?

I went in the wrong classroom. I knew as soon as I opened the door – they all burst out laughing. So I closed the door and got away as quick as I could. I felt such a fool. I didn't know what to do. I didn't dare try any other doors. I just didn't go to the lesson.

(This pupil subsequently became unable to face school at all. See *Kylie*, pp. 89–90)

If someone drops an armful of books do onlookers laugh or do they help? If someone wanders aimlessly along a corridor does the first member of staff who sees them shout at them to get to their lesson quick, or ask them if anything's wrong?

Knowledge and ideas about what's going on

How can a pupil who doesn't easily 'mix' gain access to the ideas, jokes, games and fads doing the rounds among their peers, or the issues everyone's discussing?

> The teachers used to sit on the tables at lunch. It was better – like the teacher would
> ask different people questions and everyone got a turn. Or someone would say,
> 'Do you want to hear a joke?' and – because of the teacher being there – they'd
> say it to everyone on the table and not just their friends they were sitting next to.
> I suppose it was extra work for the teachers but it was nice for us. Now it's more
> of a free-for-all. You just eat your lunch quick and get out.

During lessons pupils work alone, or if required work in twos or groups, and this is
imposed on everyone equally. But breaks, and especially the lunch-hour, can be grim.
There is a long tradition of pupils without friends spending breaks and lunchtimes
in the library. A wider range of options, lunchtime clubs, ad hoc but well-publicized
activities, things to do, which include some interaction between pupils, will make
school less socially grim for pupils who do not mix easily. They can also enable more
isolated pupils to explore ways of engaging with peers.

Having someone to talk to – feeling understood

A key component of the resolution of a pupil's difficulties in school is often the opportunity to talk to someone (see pp. 89–90). Formal counselling provision may have to be
searched for, fought for and waited for from the local education authority, local mental
health provision or some other local agency.

It may not be possible – or appropriate – to facilitate this directly from among school
staff, although informal opportunities to talk can be of immense value. Other approaches
to opening up a communication channel with a pupil who may otherwise have no-one
to share their experiences and particularly their difficulties with include mentoring and
peer support schemes. For pupils who are much more comfortable talking to adults than
peers, this last can be a particularly useful experience.

Social accomplishment[10]

As Christmas approached:

> They did this box like a letter box and everyone sent loads of cards. Then every-
> one was forever telling everyone else how many cards they'd got. And presents of
> course – there was all this present swapping. I felt like a Martian, watching it all –
> like I was the other side of this sheet of glass or something.

Occasions and activities which celebrate or rely on having friends can inadvertently hurt
and shame pupils who are loners. Making and keeping friends is a social accomplishment with which, in our society, a particular kind of social status is associated.[11] Schools
are well placed to provide structures and processes that enable pupils to interact so that
loners are not unduly disadvantaged.

> Most of the time I got by, it wasn't fun but it wasn't that bad either. Lessons were
> mostly all right. What I hated was when the teacher said to get into groups. In PE
> it's picking teams. Two or three get called up by the teacher to do it. They pick
> their friends first and then the most athletic or least useless. Until there are just

the plonkers left – like they'd rather go out low on numbers than have her or me. Actually, I think it's cruel.

This can easily be avoided:

- draw up team or group list in advance

or

- go through the class allocating A, B, C and D (or bear, lion, rhino, moose) so that all the As (or bears) form a team, all the Bs (or lions) another team and so on.

  I used to hate play-time. Just hanging around outside waiting for the bell trying to keep out of the way. But now they've got it so you can go and do some work. Or just read. They announce which classrooms are for doing school work, and you just go along. I think it's the quietness that I like.

Inclusive images

With the media you see these things . . . it will flash . . . these beautiful things, and it just stays in the back of your mind . . . I think people think, oh, I have to look like that because they think that they will have a perfect life as well. If I'm beautiful, if I'm attractive, if I'm skinny then everything else in my life has to come up as well, like my school grades will come up, I'll get a boyfriend, you know, I'll have a great social life.[12]

Even if a school wanted to, it would be unlikely to prevent its pupils reading magazines, watching TV, going to the cinema, getting their hair cut like David Beckham. But schools *can* offer pupils a broader range of images . . .

1 *Pupils of the week*: each week four or five pupils are identified for 'something nice'. Staff or peers can nominate any pupil by filling in a form (pupils need to get a member of staff to 'second' their nomination). Photos (e.g. A4 prints from a digital camera) of each week's pupils are displayed prominently and suitably captioned . . .
    Ronaldo Da Silva – *smile of the week*
    Pippa Grayling – *no-fuss hard work*
    Fatima Ihiro – *raised £42 for RSPCA – sponsored swim*
   'It was a bit sort of . . . creepy at first. But every week the photos changed and you did. . . . *see* it. It's nice. Pictures of celebrities – now I might just think, "*Airbrushed*" or . . . "*So?*" . . .'
2 *Community news*: a joint project with the local paper enabled a school to display large, photo-quality images of local news events, updated each week. Pupils were seen gathered around spotting who they knew in the pictures.
3 *Work experience*: a link with a photography course at a local college led to a large display of 'action shots' of all the Year 10 pupils on their work experience placements.

Maths rules

The type of display of mathematics and mathematicians outlined below can, of course, be worked up by any department covering any subject area. The trick is to emphasize the subject-based dimension of each person shown in the display, i.e. not to create a display of individuals who have 'overcome disability' to achieve in miscellaneous fields (see p. 13).

The display works best if it includes wide-ranging, non-hierarchical examples, with illustrations, of both the people named and a glimpse of their work.

Maths around the world . . .

Arabic numerals, themselves a modification of Hindu number notation, were adopted in Europe from about the twelfth century. This notation facilitates arithmetic in a way that Roman numerals could not.

Chinese calculators – the abacus – were invented thousand of years ago and have been in use ever since.

Babylonian algebra, in the form of quadratic equations for instance, was used to calculate quantities when engineering irrigation channels, etc. Algebra is from the arabic *al-jebr* = resetting of something broken (Babylon approximates to modern-day Iraq).

African drum rhythms . . . multiplication tables in action . . . http://echarry.web.wesleyan.edu/africother.html

Mathematicians past and present . . .

Pierre de Fermat 1601–1665   An amateur mathematician who earned his living as a lawyer and magistrate, Fermat contributed a great deal to number theory. Fermat was a modest man who refused to publish his work – it was left to others to publicize his talents. The famous 'Fermat's Last Theorem' was finally proved by the English mathematician Andrew Wiles in the 1990s.

Isaac Newton 1643–1727   One of the most influential mathematicians and physicists. His *Principia Mathematica* is the greatest scientific book ever written. His laws of physics were dominant until Einstein's general relativity 200 years later.

Carl Gauss 1777–1855   Known as the prince of mathematicians. Made major advances in most areas of mathematics. There is a famous story of a teacher at school giving his class an exercise to add up the first 100 integers, in order to keep them quiet. Gauss, aged 10, responded almost instantly with the correct answer!

Charles Babbage 1791–1871   English mathematician famous for his 'difference engine', which was the forerunner of the modern computer. A computer has recently been built based on his designs and it worked!

Emmy Noether 1882–1935 One of the founders of modern algebra, Emmy also contributed to general relativity. She had to fight descrimination against women at university. Another mathematician, Hilbert, helped her by advertising her lectures in his name!

Srinivasa Ramanujan 1887–1920 One of India's greatest mathematicians. His poor background and lack of formal education limited his opportunities in India. His genius was recognized by the English mathematician Hardy, who invited him to England and worked with him on many results in pure mathematics.

Gaston Julia 1893–1978 Julia was one of the founders of fractal/chaos theory. His brilliant paper, *Mémoire sur l'iteration des fonctions rationelles*, first published in 1918, was widely studied in the 1920s. He became a distinguished professor at the Ecole Polytechnique in Paris. His mathematical work came back into prominence in the 1970s when Mandelbrot used it in his fundamental computer experiments. (As a soldier in World War I, Julia was seriously wounded and lost his nose. He wore a leather strap across his face for the rest of his life.)

Stephen Hawking 1942– Hawking made his name developing theoretical work on black holes. He also did much to popularize physics with his book *A Brief History of Time*. Hawking has been physically disabled for many years due to motor neurone desease and comunicates by means of a speech synthesizer.

Future mathematicians

Display a large photo of members of a maths class holding up their work on Venn Diagrams. Venn Diagrams, of course, are a lovely tool for exploring the things which make us different from each other (which appear in separate regions) and the things we have in common (described by overlapping regions).

Biographies and pictures of mathematicians can be found on http://www.gap.dcs.st_and.ac.uk/~history/BiogIndex.html and mathematicians who were/are blind can be found on http://www.ams.org/notices/200210/comm_morin.pdf.

Chapter 5

Teasing, name-calling, ostracism and bullying

Seeing the problem

Children with disfigurements are twice as likely to be severely bullied as their counterparts without visible difference.[1] Many more who do not have a disfigured appearance fear teasing or bullying about appearance in school.[2] Three-quarters of children whose parents or care workers report bullying to their children's teachers found that the bullying continued or got worse.[3] Many pupils with disfigurements report feeling that staff have not taken their complaints seriously.

> If it was racist name-calling, the school would be down on it like a ton of bricks, but staring or pulling faces at me or snidy little comments or calling me Scarface, it just doesn't register with them that this is not okay.

Appearance concerns that are not linked to a disfiguring injury or condition, but merely 'normal' teenager worries about skin and hair, spots and body shape, clothes and shoes, are also apt to be dismissed as superficial or trivial concerns.

Teasing

Teasing can be subtle and almost invisible.

> There was a song called *U.G.L.Y.* by Daphne and Celeste. The lyrics were about someone being the main attraction at the zoo and *you need to see a plastic surgeon fast*. You'd wonder if it's legal. Tanya actually did have some plastic surgery coming up in the summer to revise her burn scars. I think the other girls used to hum a few notes of *U.G.L.Y.* from time to time – whenever they knew Tanya would be able to hear. Tanya tried to complain but her teachers couldn't make it out – very sensibly, they'd never listened to this horrendous so-called song.

Name calling

Name calling can target any noticeable feature (red hair, big ears, wrong trainers) and can be clever and amusing. In a classroom in Ireland, when a child with large sticking-out ears was called 'Ear Lingus' everyone including the teacher laughed – until she saw that the child concerned was holding back his tears. (The national airline, whose planes have large sticking-out wings, is called Aer Lingus.)

Ostracism

Ostracism can be hard for staff to spot:

> I wanted them in groups – which wasn't unusual but this time I was saying, 'Not three, not five, four.' Hretna was dithering at the back of the room and there was a group of three at the front near me, so I told her to come and join them. One of them immediately turned to me with, 'Oh sir no, *please* not us. We're *much better* just being three. *Please* sir, *really* we are.' Very nice, very pleasing, the way she said it. At the same time I noticed Hretna hesitating with this strange, strained sort of look on her face. How she looked was frightened. It was hardly anything and yet a penny dropped.

Bullying

Conventional bullying may be easier to spot but no easier to deal with.

> After moving up to secondary school, Carl had been verbally abused and punched in the face more than once by older boys. He'd had serious facial surgery so it was terribly dangerous for him. School staff talked about stopping it but the violence and intimidation continued. We pressed the local education authority to find him a place at another school and they were very good. He's been a different person since we got him moved – back to his old happy, keen-to-learn self. I just wish he hadn't had to go through it.

A minor incident?

> The cases of children who reported feeling suicidal or attempting suicide suggest that it is dangerous to label some forms of bullying as 'mild'. Instances of bullying dismissed by adults as trivial can fundamentally undermine a child's sense of well-being and self-esteem.[4]

Tackling bullying behaviour

What follows is not a draft policy document for pupil behaviour, but brief notes and pointers to supplement the policies, anti-bullying strategies and mechanisms for disciplining errant pupils which schools already need and have.

Receiving and acting upon reports of bullying

A pupil may go for months or years 'pretending' that everything is okay when it is not. They may be attempting to counter feeling conspicuous by avoiding any extra attention from school staff. They may not want to add to their parents' worries. They may believe that staff can't stop it happening – many teacher interventions make bullying worse.[5] Or they may have low expectations of how pleasant their school days – or their life in general – will be. A small number of children with disfigurements are disempowered through being disliked and bullied at home too.

Careful observation and regularly asking a pupil how things are going, *and paying careful attention to what they say and how they say it*, can make all the difference between months of unhappiness and 'nipping it in the bud'. A form teacher or someone with specific pastoral responsibility should see this as part of their role. If a pupil seeks them out when they are busy they must ask the pupil to wait or arrange an alternative time not too far ahead. Offloading worries is important, as is following up anything untoward that comes to light.

It can also be useful to ask other sensible and reliable pupils for their observations from time to time. How are things in the playground, in the cloakrooms, on the school bus?

Effective strategies for vulnerable pupils

These should replace any inclination to advise a pupil to 'ignore it' (often well-meant but always disempowering). Vulnerable pupils need special skills – things they can *do*. Offering to spend time with a pupil who looks different, working through the strategies, gives them important messages: they are worth it; the difficulties they are experiencing with their peers are real difficulties which can be worked on.

If 'it' happens before and after school:

- Check the route your pupil takes to school. Is there scope for an alternative?
- Can a link be engineered with supportive pupils who live near them?
- Does this pupil need to arrive and leave early or late to avoid, for instance, the start and finish times of a nearby school? To avoid making the pupil appear even more 'different', arrange for some 'buddies', or even a whole class or year, to come and go together at non-standard times.
- If 'it' happens during bus journeys to and from school discuss with the local education authority if they provide the bus service, or with the bus company who run the service. Disability discrimination legislation includes people with severe disfigurements, who are required by law to be included, not segregated, and to feel safe.

Effective strategies for all

These recognize that appearance-related teasing and bullying worry most if not all young people at school. See also Chapter 4 for more learning activities to promote enjoyment of difference across the curriculum.

Do bystanders have a role?

Pupils who 'don't do anything' consistently reinforce bullying behaviour.[6] They provide the audience: laughing, or watching mutely, or pretending it isn't happening, or feeling glad that it isn't happening to them. Pupils of primary age can show more readiness to seek teacher involvement and to support the victim, by talking with them afterwards for example. Pupils of secondary age are more able to intervene directly and less inclined to seek teacher involvement, but they can also be more reluctant to seek any involvement at all.

Schools usually provide little support to students helping others and in many cases do not reinforce those children who try to solve bully–victim conflicts. However, children need to meet with full support and positive encouragement from the school staff when providing help. Cowie (1998) suggests that schools paying attention to children's helping behaviour will be more successful than other schools in involving the peer group and enhancing behavioural changes.[7]

See p. 57 for ideas to bring this about.

Recovering children and young people who bully

If bullying persists after pupils who bully have been identified and punished, then more needs to be done and a different approach taken. There is some evidence that raising self-esteem makes people more comfortable with difference. See Chapter 6. There is not space here to go further into this considerable topic. Ideally, schools should consider drawing upon the expertise of organizations such as *Kidscape*.

Effective strategies for vulnerable pupils

Good self-talk

We all do a certain amount of 'self-talk' in our heads. Here, the task is:

1   Help the young person identify what goes through their head when they are feeling hassled about their appearance
2   Identify negative or destructive thoughts (e.g. 'I hate them').
3   Replace these with positive thoughts (good self-talk) which will calm them down and help them feel good about themselves. The pupil needs to choose something that feels right to them. 'I can handle this.'
4   Practise: when the pressure is on – walking from lesson to lesson along crowded corridors for instance – the pupil silently repeats their good self-talk.

'Me and my friends, we know how to have a good laugh.' A pupil in possession of good self-talk can appear less bothered and more self-assured. 'Ipswich Town – we win some, we lose some, but we never give up.' It can help a child not to show they're upset, and can modify the upset feeling itself. 'Not bothering to get to know me – they don't know what they're missing.' Good self-talk which specifically registers a child's efforts and achievements can help improve self-image. 'When I work hard I get results – looks like I'm going to get somewhere.'

Body language

A more positive internal sense of self or more positive emotions (good self-talk) can help a pupil find a body posture which impacts more favourably on others.[8] Non-verbal communication – the *predominant* form of communication – is crucial. See Chapter 8 for more on eye-contact and body-language.

I was just passing when Mr Gillie was about to go in to this class and you could hear it was a jungle in there. I saw him rub his hands – like *with glee* – and make himself very tall. He just looked so up for it. Then he went in and said 'Quiet please' and they did. So now I do that enthusiastic rub thing just ahead of going in to lunch, say, and I get a sort of buzz instead of that sinking feeling. I think it makes me a bit *wider* as well as taller. It makes me feel more okay and I know it shows too.

Take charge: Explain

'Explaining under fire', so to speak, may be seen as 'extreme' *Having something to say.* (see p. 22). The person who is being picked on because of their appearance has the option of taking the (absolutely valid) view that the bully is 'troubled by' their visible difference but doesn't know how to express this better. When fully prepared, rehearsed and ready, the pupil looks for a suitable opportunity to put their case, such as getting in quick before 'the usual stuff' starts up:

> Look, hang on – just because I look different doesn't mean I'm not an ordinary person just like you. I happen to have a facial difference but we're both just people really.

Self-talk, eye-contact and body-language will need to be right too. Appearing calm and 'together' when taking such an important risk requires a great deal of rehearsal and courage – and perhaps a teacher in the wings to step in if needed, or to recognize the achievement.

Importantly, this courageous approach also offers the bully some respect – it assumes that they are basically sensible.

Take charge: Humour

All the strategies set out here are 'win–win', where the erstwhile victim recasts him or herself more positively while involving no loss of face for the bully.

> [S]elf-deprecatory humour is also seen as valuable, perhaps particularly to males since Nelson-Jones (1995, p. 303) evaluates boys as *'especially prone to learning poor social skills as, more often than girls, they use words to gain social status and dominance, rather than to build bridges'*. Lefebvre and Arndt (1988) also mention a sense of humour as playing an important role in protecting against the *'helpless rage and humiliation felt in reaction to stares and name-calling'* (p. 454). They suggest that although being humorous is typically thought of as a natural talent, it is worth acquiring the skill for its social usefulness in bullying situations.[9]

'Ah well, I put my face on inside out – what can I expect?'

'And here's me, I thought it was cool to look different.'

Thorough preparation and practice are essential to achieve sure-footedness, and remove any trace of sarcasm or aggression. 'The way you stare, it's clear you cannot resist my gorgeous and original looks' could be risky. A useful guide is to refer only to oneself and say nothing at all about the bully or what s/he is saying or doing.

'My face is like a modern art original. It could be worth a fortune one day.'

'I was all the rage at Halloween!'

Fogging

The pupil with the disfigured appearance is helped to devise a range of non-aggressive follow-ons. When someone lobs a nasty or clever-dick comment in their direction they reply with some gentle fogging and then take their leave.

'Hey, wart-zone, was your father a toad?'
'Excuse me, is there a problem?'

The aim is to sound calm and collected, even vaguely interested and friendly, but puzzled by the other person's conversational gambit.

'Where did you get those amazing ears?'
'I'm sorry, I'm not sure what point you're trying to make.'

'Where did you get that face?'
'And your point is?'

Pupils report that this leaves them feeling competent and satisfied instead of harassed, powerless and humiliated.

'Alien, what planet are you from?'
'It's clear you're saying something to me but I'm not sure what it is exactly.'

If the goading persists, the pupil just persists back, gently puzzled by what the other person is trying to get at.

'You need to see a plastic surgeon.'
'I'm sorry, I'm not sure I follow you.'
'I said you need to see a plastic surgeon.'
'I'm sorry, I seem to be unclear about what you're getting at.'
'You need to see a plastic surgeon, dough-face.'
'And what is the point you're making here?'

The pupil can then leave the situation and go on their way, perhaps with a slight, perplexed shrug. The erstwhile tormentor or clever-dick is left feeling as if they have tried but failed to have a conversation. It has become a non-event. If they're tempted to have another go, it might even turn into a real conversation.

'Hey, dough-face, you still haven't seen that plastic surgeon.'
'I'm sorry I'm still not sure what you're getting at.'

'Your face, look, it's weird. What is it with your face?'

[Urgent thought: do I fog on or do I answer like it's a sensible question at last?] *'Oh, my face! Yes, I'm with you. Yes, I was attacked by a dog when I was two. Do you have a dog?'*

'A dog? Yeah, my mum has a dog. She wanted a guard-dog type but it just wags it tail.'

That was an exceptional outcome (from a pupil who had done a lot of work on *Having something to say*, see Chapter 2) but it is not unknown for tormentor and tormented to become friends. Perhaps there really is some issue which the person who bullies is struggling with and which the young person with the disfigurement manifests – and with which, just very occasionally, they can eventually show the way. Or perhaps the person who bullies just wants to be stopped in a non-humiliating way.

Rehearsing the strategies and 'going live'

A small group of peers is the ideal situation for considering typical insults and figuring out suitable responses. Everyone in the group will need to take turns at doing clever-dick comments and bully taunts, and everyone will need to take turns at reacting with whichever of the strategies they are working on. Acting tough, mouthy and dominant can, of itself, be a positive experience – a chance to re-jig anxious, harassed body-language. A good laugh can sometimes be had as well, and this, too, will do nothing but good.

When some confidence and fluency have been achieved in rehearsal, the time comes to 'go live'. Great courage is required. Like acting, it is not just pretending but 'getting into the character' of someone who doesn't let bullying behaviour get to them. Gradually it becomes real and unfriendly taunts do stop getting to them so much.

Some structure is needed to meet the challenge of 'going live' and survive the inevitable set-backs. Table 5.1 gives an example for planning and self-review.

Having somewhere to go

Children who are teased or bullied are often advised to avoid their tormentors. 'Go and find someone else to play with/talk to.' This can be very difficult for a pupil who is in the uncomfortable position of not having friends. 'Just walk away.' Children in groups are far less likely to be bullied.[10] Wandering around the playground as if in search of non-existent friends can make a pupil even more vulnerable to their assailants.

Learning how to make and keep friends is a long-term project (see Chapters 6, 7 and 8). In the meantime, and for pupils whose nature is more solitary, schools need to organize somewhere for such children to go.

Vulnerable (but not necessarily bookish) pupils who head for the library know this on some level. They may be lucky – perhaps there are library monitors or an easy-going, occasionally conversational librarian. Or they may merely practise being quiet – talking even less to others than they already do.

A more positive recourse is to set up some kind of 'cool corner' or 'buddy bench' furnished with one or more pupils who are briefed to 'be available'. They are usually older pupils, sensible, and sociable. They might rota their 'cool corner' stints, and organize the whole thing themselves, with a member of staff just quietly in the background monitoring how it's going.

Table 5.1 How I mastered queues and corridors

Strategy	Example scripts	Rehearsals	How did it go?	Queues & corridors	How did it go?
Good self-talk	I can handle this. I'm a good mate and my mates are good mates too.	14.2.01 18.2.01 6.3.01	Glazed over 2/10 Still a bit glazed 5/10 Got it 10/10	13.3.01	Very nervous and self conscious. Don't think this showed. 7/10
Body language	Think tall, think cool.	14.2.01 18.2.01 6.3.01			
Take charge/explain	Look, it's just a cleft. It doesn't bother me, don't let it bother you.	14.3.01			
Take charge/humour	I guess maybe I was too enthusiastic with my spoon when I was learning to eat.				
Fogging	I'm sorry, I'm not getting this. No, I'm still not getting your point here. And your point is?				

Their job is simply to 'be there', a friendly presence. They might strike up a conversation (though not about being bullied). Lessons, homework, computer games, what was on TV last night. Or tell jokes. Pupils, formerly at risk of being alone and exposed, now have somewhere to 'hang out' – *people to hang out with.*

This approach can be incorporated into good self-talk (see above). As harassment looms, 'I can choose to spend my time with people I like.'

Time spent in company at a cool corner can help to promote social confidence and contribute to developing social skills. It is likely to be rewarding in itself. However, it will be worth remarking to a vulnerable pupil when they adopt this strategy that they have made a good choice.

Effective strategies for all

Many widely applicable practical approaches have been developed for resolving difficulties between pupils so that the victims of bullying are not put at risk and the pupils who bully are not themselves shamed or humiliated. The learning activities described here are ideal for Drama or PSHE (Personal, Social and Health Education).

Make more time for everyone's appearance concerns

There is some evidence that young people realize that it is their own preoccupation with looks, bodyshape, hair, skin and fashion that makes them vulnerable and unhappy. 'The media portrays the image of girls, how we want to be, like skinny or whatever, and I don't know it just kind of takes over . . . we don't think properly . . . we forget other things, like we don't think about inside, like personality and the inner self.'[11] But knowing this does not mean that appearance concerns can be suddenly and refreshingly cast aside.

Teenagers worry about teasing and bullying about appearance, and about their own lack of confidence with those who look different from themselves.[12] Appearance concerns affect academic performance – deciding, for instance, not to speak up in class unless they feel good about their appearance.[13] 'If I look bad I won't go into town or be in school. I stay at home and watch TV.'[14]

Learning activities which focused on appearance concerns rather than dismissing them as trivial had very significant outcomes.[15]

1   Pupils complete a questionnaire about how much and in what ways they worry about how they look.
2   In groups led mainly by older pupils (rather than teachers), pupils learn several distinct and specific strategies for dealing with appearance-related bullying. The basic strategies had been specifically developed by *Changing Faces* to help children and young people with facial disfigurements to deal more effectively with appearance-related hassle from others. They are similar to those listed here on pp. 51–2.

Both immediately after, and six months after the intervention, pupils scored significantly higher on some important questions, compared with scores before the intervention, and scores for the control group.

How confident are you to approach someone who looks very different from you?
How confident are you to advise friends who are teased or bullied about appearance?
How confident are you to speak up in class?

Thus it appears that this 'skills training for appearance-related-hassle' made pupils more socially inclusive, more supportive of each other and more motivated in lessons. Their self-esteem also benefited.

Giving bystanders a clear role

Children are often asked by adults to behave nicely and sociably. But inconsistency between words and deeds fills the child's world. Empathy, role-models and social approval are more important determinants in the development of helping behaviour support.[16]

The video *How was your day?*[17] shows a day in the school life of two students, one girl, one boy, who were bullied. Parents', teachers' and peers' reactions are shown too. After the video, useful areas for class discussion include:

> What can you gather from the video about the inner qualities of these two young people? What are they *like* as people? (Never pass up an opportunity to practise this vital inclusion skill!)
> What kinds of peer reactions (including silence, laughing, etc.) support or endorse bullying behaviour?
> What kinds of peer reactions (getting a teacher, befriending the victim, intervening to dissuade the bully or protect the victim, etc.) discourage bullying behaviour?
> Are there rules about what 'bystanders' should or shouldn't do that it would be useful to have in class/in school?
> Are there things the 'bystanders' could do that haven't been thought of yet? (Use role-play to try out different scenarios and see how different peer responses affect bully, victim and the peer(s) themselves.)
> How will school staff view such bystander reactions? What could teachers do/not do that would help non-involved classmates to respond positively?

A school council discussion involving teacher representatives, or a staff discussion involving pupil representatives, may follow. Peer involvement can be very effective but children and young people do need to be well-prepared and well-supported by school staff.

What if a pupil with a disfigurement is aggressive or provocative?

Is staring hostile?

Understanding other people's reactions to anyone who looks 'different' is an essential foundation stone that may be missing. This can leave a pupil who looks different feeling enraged by the unwanted attention they get and over which they have no control. See *How to stop staring* on pp. 20–1 and *Having something to say* p. ??

Do they know how to be good?

A pupil with facial disfigurement may have had, from an early age, 'mixed messages' about how to behave.[18] Acceptable behaviour may need to be 'taught' and consistently rewarded.

> When Garry's Mum said goodbye, she told him to be good. But when I asked him what being good meant he didn't seem to know. So I talked about walking quietly along the corridor with our arms at our sides and we did this together all the way round the school. Twice, once fast and once slow. Like training for some kind of school marathon! Before, he'd always been told off – ineffectually – for jumping about and shouting with his arms all over the place and sometimes hitting other children in the process. Now we can say, 'Show me that lovely quiet walking you do so well.'

What are they not managing to communicate more appropriately?

A child who is facially disfigured may need help to identify and name the feeling(s) that seem to be linked to 'losing it' (see Chapter 8). Until they are able to stop and say something before they erupt, they may only be able to recognize that they are getting very fired up, in which case 'time out' in some pre-arranged setting within the school may be necessary. It is vital to involve other teachers to ensure uniformity of approach. It can also be helpful to share concerns and work jointly with parents.

Who started it?

A child with a disfigurement may be reacting to 'almost invisible' (to staff) teasing or bullying (see p. 48). It is essential to check this out thoroughly and act effectively. A pupil who has a disfigurement and is at risk of 'taking the law into her own hands' needs to know that 'the law' is alive and well in the hands it belongs in. Alongside this, however, you can guide them towards more effective strategies (see pp. 51–5) and work with them to reduce their sense of isolation, powerlessness or frustration.

All pupils (and staff) need a clear picture of what behaviour is unacceptable. Even if the school endorses appropriate 'bystander' responses, everyone should understand the importance of reporting to a member of staff every instance of unkind teasing (teasing which is not enjoyed by the person being teased), name-calling, ostracism or bullying, however threatening the aggressor or trivial the incident.

Chapter 6

Self-esteem

Taking care of self-esteem

Self-esteem may be or become an issue for any child or young person who has an injury or condition that affects the way they look. However, it is also true that someone with no disfigurement can have painfully low self-esteem and someone with a severe facial disfigurement can have very good self-esteem. Deteriorating self-esteem has been linked to people's repeated failure to achieve their desired level of social interaction, and/or their repeated failure to achieve smooth-running social interactions.[1]

This is not to say that a pupil's appearance concerns can be discounted. Many teenagers and, increasingly, younger children too, may express dissatisfaction with their appearance – to the point of staying away from school when they don't feel confident of the way they look.[2] Adults are apt to dismiss this as an unnecessary or superficial preoccupation. But much teasing, name-calling and bullying takes the form of appearance-related comments or taunts. There is also a clear association between appearance-related concern and low self-esteem[3]. So how is one to respond if a child or young person with a visible difference expresses concern that they don't look how they used to, or how they wish they did, or don't look like everyone else, or that they just don't like the way they look? After all, their initial social interactions tend to be hard going and their conversations can falter because the other person is disconcerted by their unusual appearance.

Here are four aspects, then, to consider when addressing self-esteem:

- talking about what we look like
- managing social interactions
- standing up to teasing, name-calling and bullying
- identifying low self-esteem
- repairing damaged self-esteem.

Talking about what we look like

> 'My Mum, people at school, everyone – they're always telling me I look fine. In the end how I feel is I don't believe *anything* they say any more.' (Carrie has a cleft lip and palate.)

Families and children may not have words for a condition or its treatment or for the child's appearance. 'This can . . . lead to a taboo in talking about appearance.' Children are unable to answer questions and are 'reluctant to talk to their parents about their concerns.'[4] If no-one ever talks to a child about their appearance, *including the scarring or asymmetry or skin texture or unusual features that make them 'different'*, then they will have no starting place for dealing with the staring, comments or teasing, or with their sense that they do look different. In short, they become powerless and isolated. *Having something to say* (see Chapter 2) is a vital component of tackling low self-esteem.

> I don't remember anyone ever saying anything except medical sort of things about my scars until I got to university. We were sitting around having coffee, a load of us, all new, just getting to know each other. This boy was looking hard at my arms, and then he said, 'Your skin, I hope you don't mind if I say this, your skin is like a galaxy, you know the way the stars all swirl. It's so interesting. It's lovely.' It was a great day in my life, to hear someone say that.

Managing social interactions

Every kind of social interaction is relevant here.

The briefest encounters, such as passing someone you vaguely know in a doorway, may seem trivial – but can be an added source of social anxiety for any child or young person with a disfigurement. '*Smile and say Hi*' might be a good rule, but not necessarily an easy one to follow. For a pupil with a disfigurement, past experiences of being stared at or turned away from may have 'taught' them to take evasive action rather than attempt social interaction. If a pupil tends to keep their head down or keep their gaze averted in such situations, it maybe useful to check out how they are feeling when they walk around the school. Then it may be appropriate to do some skills training to enable the pupil to feel and look more self-assured. See good self-talk and body language pp. 50–1. From this improved position, it becomes easier to receive a greeting and nod a response. Thus brief but perhaps stressful situations which can occur many times each day, may be turned into more positive social interactions which actually benefit the pupil's self-esteem.

Meeting new people, holding conversations or just *hanging out* together are key challenges for anyone who looks different. *Having something to say* (p. 22) sets out the specialized social skills and understanding which enable children and young people to deal with other people's preliminary reactions to their appearance so that they can get to know each other as people. Chapter 7 on *social skills* looks at more social interactions in more contexts. If children and young people can have and enjoy the kind of social experiences they want, as often as they want, this will help to maintain or improve their self-esteem.

Chapter 5 sets out a range of strategies for tackling hassle from other pupils. Being empowered in this way has been shown to raise self-esteem.[5]

Recognizing and understanding the things children with low self-esteem do to try and cope (which can include *seeming very confident*) can help to avoid further lowering their self-esteem by tackling these *symptoms* or *coping strategies head-on*. The section below on identifying low self-esteem describes sometimes difficult and even 'self-destructive' behaviours often seen by teachers (and parents). Attempts to tackle these behaviours directly can further lower self-esteem. By carefully identifying whether a pupil has lowered self-esteem, school staff can improve the likelihood that the situations can be substantially improved by integrating measures to manage unacceptable behaviours into a more radical programme to raise self-esteem.

Repairing damaged self-esteem forms the main part of this chapter. Perhaps this section could be seen as forming the basis for a set of guidance notes for all staff in all schools (and their managers!) – just maximizing everyone's self-esteem tends to promote social inclusion, because people with high self-esteem find difference easier to manage.

Identifying low self-esteem

The following (counterproductive) coping strategies have been associated with low self-esteem. These are the things which children most often do to try and escape from their sense of their own failure, weakness, incompetence, etc.

Quitting   Can't seem to succeed, so 'This is boring', they give up. A child may develop a pattern of moving aimlessly (or energetically) from one activity to another with little real engagement in any task.

Avoiding   Like quitting, but before even starting the task or activity. Either 'up front' in a surly or jeering way, or more subtly with plausible excuses, especially 'Been there. Done that. We did it last year, Miss.' A pupil may suddenly prefer some other activity, or become stubborn, or make excuses.

Cheating   Alter or dodge the rules, explicitly or privately, but protest innocence (or ignorance) if challenged. A child for whom being seen to do anything but win means being seen to fail, may appear 'sneaky' or may start pointing out things the 'referee' should have seen. Everything but their own ascendancy is criticized as 'not fair'.

Clowning and regressing   Maybe done to gain more control by getting attention for something of their own choosing instead of whatever it is they want to distract you *and their peers* from. A child who, in the playground, gets called names to do with her appearance (which is beyond her control) might be relieved to be called 'Nuisance' or to be told she's 'Spoiling it for everyone' for something she has actually *done*. A child whose low self-esteem means he can't remember anything he's good at, might find himself telling jokes about constipated mathematicians when confronted with yet another too-hard maths exercise, to reduce the seeming importance of a task.

Controlling   Attempting to dictate to others (parents, siblings, peers), to compensate for the lack of control they feel in situations in which failure occurs. This may come across as being interfering or bossy or patronising.

Being critical, aggressive or bullying   To hide own feelings of inadequacy by belittling or scapegoating others.

Being passive-aggressive   A pupil agrees or even offers to do something but does not, and then says 'I forgot.' It leaves others feeling messed around.

Denying   To avoid the pain which would result from acknowledging their limitations or vulnerabilities a pupil might react to an important task with 'Don't care.' Or deny that they are worried about a project assignment, or deny that they did not/could not do their homework but instead have 'lost it'.

> *Rationalizing* Making excuses for poor performance rather than accepting respons-
> ibility, especially by *externalizing*, i.e. blaming other people, things or events. A
> child who feels their disfigurement stigmatizes them will tend to attribute the
> negative behaviour of other people to the stigmatizing condition, often incor-
> rectly.[6] He gets told off because he's shouting out in class – nothing to do with
> his burn scars. They don't invite her to join them for a game of pool because she
> always pots the cue-ball – nothing to do with her eczema.
>
> *Being impulsive* This may be a characteristic of a child's temperament, but can
> also be a way of coping – by tackling a task too quickly 'just to get it over
> with'.

Even though these coping strategies are clearly counter productive, they were originally
developed by the child in an attempt to manage a dreadful sense of failure or imperfec-
tion and to maintain (subjectively) a sense of dignity. Lack of control in social situations
– being stared at – can lead to a terrible sense of powerlessness and failure. The way
forward therefore is to teach the child strategies for *dealing with* unwanted attention and
to (re)build their self-esteem. Forbidding or punishing the unsatisfactory coping behaviour
may entrench rather than remove it, by further lowering self-esteem. Setting achievable
targets for alternative behaviours will be more effective (see below).

A further factor in tackling these problems effectively is that low self-esteem
brings with it an increased tendency to take negative experiences and comments to
heart while becoming more resistant to positive signs from others. The teacher's task
becomes to notice and mention the positives without 'trumpeting' or the pupil's guard
will be alerted and the teacher's words will be dismissed as some kind of contrived and
valueless 'compliment' or as some sort of charity. 'Nice work,' and straight onto the
next pupil, may be more effective than 'Osama, you're writing's so improved, well
done.' This should always be said without a trace of irony or sarcasm (see below).

Strategies and interventions promoting self-esteem

These are most effective if the child or young person experiences them consistently
over several months throughout the school day and also at home. So it is important to
involve parents and colleagues and agree a self-esteem building programme which is
understood by and involves them all.

Attunement

Staff need to review their own adjustment to this pupil's unusual or changed appearance (see Chapter 1). *What would it be like to spend a day in their shoes?* For example, all
staff, but especially PE staff, should ensure that teams are never selected one at time
by nominated captains – they pick friends and favourites first and those who are left
until last suffer great pain. Sarcasm, euphemism and patronization all tend to emphasize
the powerlessness of the person on the receiving end and it is essential to avoid them.
Anyone who finds the pupil being supported 'difficult to like' can find it useful to ask
among colleagues for more informed and positive impressions – and then try to 'spot'
for themselves what colleagues have tuned in to.

Modelling

A professional style which explicitly models desired behaviours is often more effective, long term, than a reactive approach which criticizes and corrects. It can be particularly helpful if staff can occasionally model acknowledging a difficulty and making the effort to overcome it. 'It gets hard to concentrate, doesn't it, towards the end of a lesson. Do you find that? I have to really push myself sometimes to keep on task.' 'I think I may have misunderstood you. I'm sorry. Would you mind explaining it again to me?' Over time, this will tend to help a pupil not only to see how a problem (in this case a misunderstanding) might be resolved, but to learn that acknowledging a difficulty and then putting it right need involve no loss of face.

Mistakes are just information

A good learning environment releases pupils from the need to guard anxiously against mistakes and failures. Successes are best registered in terms of the effort and risk ventured by the pupil (never luck), and failure as risk taken, what can be learnt from it, and what could be done differently next time?

Even a pupil's tendency to make apparently careless slips when they are otherwise working well may be due to a fear of being too slow or not getting finished. They will learn best how to make the compromise between speed and accuracy from adults who are comfortable with their own necessary compromises.

Separate actions from people

What a pupil has done or is doing must never be confused with who they are as a person. Ideally concern over a pupil's unsatisfactory action or outcome should be combined with a more positive comment about them as a person or about something else they've done. 'I'm surprised you've mislaid your homework, you're often quite on-the-ball in my lessons.' Pupils should never be given nick names or negative labels – not even 'affectionately' (Here comes trouble!) or in a teacher's private thoughts!

Middle way

The task here is to be neither overprotective of ('He won't be able to cope') nor aggressive toward ('She's got to cope') the pupil you are working with. It can help to check: 'Are you okay showing these visitors round on your own? Or would you like to go with someone who's done it before?"

Target strengths

Identifying a pupil's temperament, interests, and aptitudes may require careful observation by staff, especially if the pupil resorts to clowning or quitting to avoid their pervasive sense of failure or powerlessness. Positive moments or actions must be noticed and acknowledged if possible – but in an authentic, low-key manner as mentioned above. 'You have quite an eye for colour.' 'Thanks for remembering to water the plants, poor things. I'd quite forgotten.'

Find a role

How can this pupil's school experiences be extended to give them opportunities to take a little more responsibility, make a contribution, and experience useful involvement? Obviously, their capabilities need to be matched and not belittled or overstretched. Reorganizing the desks for small groups, helping to carry stuff . . . Many children and young people with disfigurements, especially if they have spells in hospital, may prefer to talk to adults than peers so it can be useful to pair the pupil with a classmate for this, rather than appear to be assuming or cultivating a particular staff–pupil bond.

Create choices

Clear, manageable opportunities for making choices and decisions, solving problems and generally getting a handle on things are very important. Especially around the pupil's least favourite, least successful tasks (where they are most likely to revert to a counter-productive coping strategy) they will feel more in control if there is an element of choice. 'Will you write in your exercise book or would you rather put your answers straight on the worksheet?' 'What's going to be better for this, pencil or pen?'

Positive focus

Encouragement and positive feedback is vital, and, wherever possible, *ignoring* the bad is important too. 'This looks good. Well done' (*no sarcasm*) following no comment at all on the previous, horribly scrappy page you got in last time. What is to be said when the pupil whose low self-esteem is in hand, and whose visible difference may make them hate feeling noticed, surprises their teacher by showing up on time for your lesson? 'Hullo Sam, Ravi, Chris' so that they are simply included (nothing special) in the greeting as they come in with the others.

Link action to results

Clear, manageable targets are essential, along with real, consistent consequences. The pupil needs to be fully involved in agreeing practical and achievable goals, and in the monitoring of their progress. 'Mrs Betts and Mr Khan are both pleased with your homework, but Miss Hall says she hasn't had anything in from you yet. How's it going? How many of these boxes are we going to tick this week?' Regular, well-informed reviews are crucial, not only for staff to keep tabs on a difficult or worrying pupil, but very importantly to help the pupil to *experience* how their own decisions and actions can make a difference.

A realistic aim may be to obtain staff agreement to a 'Self-esteem repair regime'. Identify a short list of activities/situations which seem to cause repeated difficulty and which it may be practical to avoid, or ignore, or substitute with something else, for a fixed period of time (e.g. a term). Also identify a short list of activities or experiences where there is some evidence that the pupil can perform positively. If possible, match these so that staff can 'do something' rather than being asked merely to 'stop doing something'.

Case study

Jamie had been 'a handful' but also a 'good worker' at primary school, and had transferred to secondary school with several of his classmates. His scarring from a scald in infancy had never been an issue at school. During Year 7 his work and behaviour deteriorated. Early in Year 8 his mother contacted the school, concerned that he was becoming unkind to his younger sister and to the family's two pets. She felt that this was 'caused' by her trying to make him to do his homework. She was also concerned that, over the last year, Jamie seemed to have fallen out with everyone he had transferred with from primary school, and had not made any new friends.

The Head of Year called a meeting of staff involved with Jamie, and invited mum along. Jamie was *not* present, as the very things which he was finding most painful and difficult needed to be thoroughly discussed and explored. Staff generally described Jamie as immature, idle and a constant source of distraction and irritation to others, though his Geography, CDT (Craft, Design and Technology) and Maths teachers viewed him more positively.

Out of this came the 'Self-esteem repair regime' shown below. With modifications at regular intervals, this ran from December through to July.

Self-esteem repair regime for Jamie Shah

The following guidance has been agreed following a meeting with Jamie's parents. The aim is to improve his behaviour which has been increasingly difficult both in some lessons and at break, and to improve behaviour at home too. When teaching Jamie, or when on break duty, or should you encounter him in any situation in school, especially because of 'trouble', please observe the following guidelines as closely as possible. Reviews are to be held each month and we expect the 'self-esteem repair regime' to operate until July.

Try to cut back on . . .	*. . . and instead*
pressing Jamie to work more quietly	pass small positive comments as frequently as possible, e.g. give him a smile whenever he works consistently for even just a minute or two *
generally applied homework	at end of lesson, draw up a short list of alternative specific tasks. Jamie to tick (now or later) which one he will do for homework – and then hand this one in
written work requirements	drawings, diagrams, charts, etc.

* Please avoid 'If you can do work this good today, why not every day?' (tempting though it is!)

Jamie might like to help a classmate (but probably not Kevin. Rees or Ryan Rush, even if they seem keen!) to produce a good quality chart or diagram. Ideal opportunity for this may be if someone is absent and has work to catch up on – for example, photocopy any good work of Jamie's to give them.

Figure 6.1 Jamie's self-esteem repair regime

Breaks, lunchtimes   If Jamie is loafing and at risk of 'winding up' anyone, try engaging him in conversation. Possible topics – forthcoming London trip to the Science Museum, sister Susie's recent diagnosis of diabetes, Man United, the new rabbit hutch he is designing and building, forthcoming plastic surgery to revise scars at neck.

Next progress review: 14.1.99

Thanks everyone.
Sarah Lant
Head Year 8

Figure 6.1 continued

Also, during these months, the CDT teacher agreed to introduce Jamie to a series of workbooks[7] and help him work through them. The workbooks offer ideas for understanding and dealing with staring and other seemingly 'hostile' reactions to unusual appearance, and also explore vocabulary for talking about appearance and a chance to check out inner qualities.

Improvements were slow to materialize at first. Mum reported improvements at home before anything was obviously happening at school, although he wrote up his rabbit hutch building exploits at some length for an English assignment, including several photographs. After the PE team took a small Year 8 group to see Man United play Aston Villa, Jamie formed a 'civilized' friendship with a well-motivated lad in another form. As Year 9 approached, staff were considering whether to swap Jamie or the other lad, to place them in the same form.

Chapter 7

Social skills for life

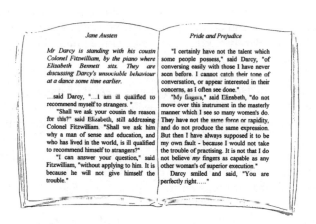

Figure 7.1 Extract from Jane Austen's *Pride and Prejudice*

Getting an overview

Normal toddlers indicate a preference for interacting with other normal toddlers, seeking them as partners and more often rejecting social initiations from handicapped children . . . parents, fearing social failures for their children . . . contribute to [their children's social inhibition] by being overprotective . . . mothers ignored their handicapped children during free play at a much greater rate than did mothers of . . . normal toddlers . . . significantly, the five most ignored children all had facial rather than orthopaedic anomalies . . .[1]

Children have an effect on one another's behaviour from as early as infancy. Distress often follows the . . . crying of an infant peer, and babies display some reciprocal touch during interaction . . . In toddlerhood . . . communication between peer dyads [explores] both co-operation and resistance to the other's overtures.
. . . [As children learned] to recognise and value one another's personal qualities . . . peers gained power as personality shaping agents . . .
. . . Peers . . . help children understand the constructs of co-operation and competition, and social roles such as deference and dominance . . . children gained a more complex understanding of social relationships as the concepts of equality, mutuality and reciprocity became central to their own close friendships. Once acquired

between friends, these concepts were . . . extended to other relationships . . . peer interaction, especially playing games, was . . . crucial to the development of children's perceptions of the self in relation to others . . . communication, conflict and role-playing in early and mid-childhood can improve perspective-taking skills and lead to decreases in aggression. . . . peers . . . [decrease] inappropriate behaviour by punishing or ignoring it and [increase] desirable activities through reinforcement . . . altruism has been shown to increase as a result of peer tutoring . . . [T]he modification of . . . aggressive or sex-typed behaviours . . . [resulted from] mere exposure to peer models . . . social withdrawal at both 5 and 7 years of age was shown to be predictive of depression and/or loneliness at 11 years of age.[2]

The school reports quite positively – everything's okay, the child has settled in, 'they are accepted' . . . But when we go in and do our own research, it emerges that these children do not have any friends. Hardly anyone ever talks to the child, they're not joining in, no-one wants to sit next to them. . . .[3]

Most children who are visibly different have an increased experience of medical concern and medical intervention. Doctors and nurses, speech and language therapists – encounters with concerned adults who have a professional interest in the child's well-being may outnumber and outweigh the child's encounters with peers who want the toy they've got or want to tell them something rather than ask them something about their health or their treatment. Different-looking children tend to have far fewer opportunities to develop 'those skills that are derived from social exchanges of conflict, communication and co-operation'.[4]

Children with disfigurements are less popular, have fewer friends – decreasing with age. These findings are surprisingly consistent across various facial disfigurements.[5] This is a particular cause for concern as people with facial disfigurements (both from birth and acquired) who coped well were very clear that friends as well as family were important factors which supported their resilience.[6] They also cited social skills including openness, non-verbal communication and humour.

Without social skills and the social experiences which they open up, a pupil's perspective can become overshadowed by their experience of disfigurement. Acquiring better social skills later enabled this person to discover 'that the anxiety that I went through [in adolescence] . . . wasn't just all down to having a cleft, that people who in my perception might have had a normal face had problems.'[7]

Individuals with strong social skills are viewed more favourably than those with poor social skills and these reactions are polarized by disfigurement.[8]

	Person with disfigurement	Person without disfigurement
Person showing good social skills	Viewed very favourably by others	Viewed fairly favourably by others
Person showing poor social skills	Viewed very unfavourably by others	Viewed fairly unfavourably by others

Everyone can benefit from better social skills, but people with disfigurements can benefit most of all. Extroversion and introversion may be seen as deeply laid personal traits, but social skills are knowledge and behaviour which people learn and acquire. For some, this happens without much conscious effort, through simply 'being with' family and friends who are socially skilled. If not, as Mr Darcy (whose social skills training is not, unfortunately, described by Jane Austen) and many participants of *Changing Faces* social skills workshops have discovered, they can be learnt. Later, they typically report 'realizing how I can actually deal with the situation and where I need to improve'.[9]

Case study
Chad (11 years old) got into trouble almost every day at school. Sometimes he protested that other pupils had wound him up and the thump he landed them was well-deserved. But teachers also observed, in corridors between lessons and out in the playground, that Chad would just go running towards another pupil and crash into them or bash them in some other way. When asked why, he said, 'I was playing.' Needless to say, most of his peers worked hard at avoiding him.

'It's as if he wants to be sociable but doesn't now how to do it. Far too physical. Somehow we've got to teach him to *say* something instead.'

Unfortunately, no-one was available to give this the time it required. Chad's enjoyment of lessons was gradually overshadowed by the aggravation that too often flared around him between lessons. Eventually, he refused to go to school at all.

Children who experience few opportunities for positive social contact have few opportunities to learn appropriate social behaviours than their more sociable peers. Children who do not, for various reasons, interact with their peers in normal ways, quantitatively and qualitatively, may be at risk of problems in the social–cognitive, social–behavioural, and even academic domains.[10]

Being without friends means that there is no-one apart from family with whom to go to the swimming pool, go into town, sit in cafes or hang out in parks with. Hence, some young people felt strongly that the quality of time spent out of school depended on relationships with other young people in school.[11] School is the main setting for most of a child's social experiences outside their family. Creating opportunities to consider social situations and rehearse strategies is a real possibility at school. Getting it right socially at school can have a very positive impact on a pupil's wider experiences outside school, and can last long after they've left school.

The following pages can be used to help a pupil who has a disfigured or distinctive appearance to consider a range of situations they may meet from time to time. The suggestions which follow each numbered *situation* are there to set the tone and establish the expectation of a positive outcome. Imagining scenarios, anticipating difficulties and practising the process of coming up with something to say, will help to avoid some of the worst knocks. Children and young people with disfigurements often do not know anyone else who shares first-hand experiences of these awful moments. Again, working through the examples with a small group of friends can help with getting a response that sounds really good. It can also help to build bonds of empathy and support among friends.

Getting to know people better and enabling them to get to know you better – making friends

Regarding encounters between different-looking and 'normal'-looking individuals Goffman notes:

> [T]he 'visibly' stigmatized [individual] . . . will have special reasons for feeling that mixed social situations make for anxious . . . interaction. But if this is so, then it is to be suspected that we normals will find these situations shaky too . . .
> [The visible difference is either] responded to . . . overtly and tactlessly . . . or, as is more commonly the case, no explicit reference is made to it . . . accompanied by one or more of the familiar signs of discomfort and stickiness: the guarded references, the common everyday words suddenly made taboo, the fixed stare elsewhere, the artificial levity, the compulsive loquaciousness, the awkward solemnity.[12]

Chapter 2 looked at the problem of staring, and the strategies which children and young people who look different can use to manage other people's initial reactions – special social skills for being out and about in public and the first moments of brief or transitory social encounters such as buying a ticket or queuing in a shop.

Here we will look at more evolved social skills where the new people encountered are going to be there tomorrow and the day after. The basic social understanding and social strategies – 'tools' – are an essential foundation. They can facilitate toleration of the extra looking that the other person can't help doing – instead of an understandable but unrealizable desire to prevent this. They establish a way of getting started when the urge to stare has jarred the other person's ordinary social skills into silence or embarrassed effusions.

Situation 1   You're new or someone else is new, such as starting at a new school or someone new joining your year group at school. Or it could be at a youth club, martial arts society, drama club, the supermarket where you work weekends.

'Hi, my name's Harjit. Excuse my weird face. You can ask me about it if you like. What's your name?'

'If you stare, you have to say hello, right? I'm Amanda, who're you?'

Situation 2   It's the geography field trip and someone gets told to sit next to you who clearly doesn't want to. Or maybe you get told to sit next to them. *'Oh no, not him.'*

'You're okay, I'm not going to attack you. I'm just going to listen to my Walkman. But if you want to borrow any of my tapes you're going to have to act nice, right?'

Situation 3   You're on holiday with your family. You're going to be there for two weeks. You want to have a good time. You want no-one to notice, like no-one notices any-more at school.

'You think I look weird? – it's cool to be weird. Tell me something about you that's weird?'

Eye-contact, body language and voice tone which are relaxed and self-assured may need further training and practice if there are any doubts in this area. Simple answers to initial questions – both asked and unasked – are important too. As they get older, children and young people need to have more and different answers.

'It's eczema. You can't catch it.'

'It's eczema and it makes my skin dry. You can't catch it.'

'It's just when your skin is really dry. Called eczema. It's not that uncommon. Have you ever had a patch of eczema?'

(In the swimming pool) 'I know I look a bit boiled but you're okay – it didn't happen in this pool!'

'It's eczema. I have to keep piling on the cream like some sort of exotic cake. A layer of ice-cream would be a relief in this weather. Do you fancy an ice-cream? There's a van round the corner. We can still see if the bus comes and run for it.'

In situations where a new acquaintance and perhaps a new friend might be made, more than *Having something to say* may be required. Similarity is a basic component of friendship[13] so if similarities are harder to 'see', how are friends to be made? Children and young people who are visibly different (and all their classmates – see Chapter 4) need to have a lively awareness of all the personal qualities, interests and experiences that make them who they are and which – since some features of their appearance may tend to set them apart – can help them to establish some common ground with other people.

Children and young people can gain much from exploring social situations through play or drama. See Figure 7.2 where Ganda and Rory meet for the first time in an improvised cartoon:

1   Rory's obviously learnt and practised *Having something to say*, and the good eye-contact and lively tone that go with it. The giraffe can't tell whether he's a really confident rhino, or just acting friendly. Maybe Rory doesn't know either any more.
2   Ganda isn't exactly gushing, but at least she observes the basic rules of politeness. Perhaps Rory's up-beat acknowledgement of his alarmingly pointy nose helps her stay tuned.
3   Ah – it looks like no-one told Rory off in the past for asking these kind of personal questions about unusual appearance.
4   Fortunately, Ganda doesn't seem put out by the question – presumably she's been stared at or asked before, or maybe she herself has noticed that most of the others have much shorter necks – and wasn't told they were rude for asking or that she was just imagining their stares, when she queried this at school.
5   Rory has actually listened to what she said . . . and he knows how to build on it.
6   This is good news indeed. They may become friends.

1 Hello, my name's Rory. Don't mind my nose
It's just the way it is. What is your name?

2 I'm Ganda. Hi!

3 Ganda, why's your neck so long?

4 It's a gene I guess. It helps me look out for lions
and eat the leaves off tall trees.

5 Is that what you eat? I eat grass and things
like that.

6 I guess we're both vegetarians then.

Figure 7.2 Rory and Ganda meet for the first time

It's quite possible that Rory, like Chad in the case study on p. 69, used to be much more rough and even accidentally hurt people in his unschooled enthusiasm to be sociable. For children whose social initiations are inappropriate (too physical, too noisy, too nosy, too tentative) careful work is required to enable them to learn and practise the right kind of 'rules' for different kinds of situations.

Unfortunately the 'rules' can be elusive. Certain words and turns of phrase can be 'cool' for a while, and then turn 'sad'. 'High-fives' and other gestures may suddenly be 'naff'. If a small group of children can be set up to help, there is a greater chance of getting the 'rules' right. Children who learn their social skills mainly from talking with education or health professionals may be at risk of sounding older than their years, or 'quaint' or 'square' – but it might not be called 'square' any more but something else the grown-ups haven't cottoned on to yet.

It can be useful to use a 'log' to plan and monitor 'social initiations' (see Table 7.1).

Being with friends who may be unfamiliar with the way strangers react

A child or young person who has learnt *Having something to say* and perhaps some of the social skills outlined above, will sometimes need to 'extend them sideways' – to manage for both themselves and whoever they are with when they encounter people who haven't seen them before.

Situation 4 Going with friends to a McDonald's for someone's birthday
Beforehand: Did you ever wonder what it would be like to be a film star? Well, when we step through this door, you'll know. Some folks just stares and stares like they've got a problem with their eyes and eyes. Ready?

Table 7.1 Planning and monitoring social interactions: a social skills planner/log

Situation	What I could try	Dates of attempts	How did it go?
Science lessons with Mr Khan – when we do an experiment in pairs.	Don't hang about worrying – go and ask someone to be my partner (e.g. Ollie Smith who has an Ipswich Town pencil case).	3.10.02 I asked Ollie. We had to test what dissolved and what didn't.	Ollie's gutted about Ipswich being relegated. So am I. We both hate Man.U. He's never been to a match.
New neighbours at home – moved in last month. Two children, girl and boy, I don't know their names.	When they go out the front and play on their bikes I could take my skateboard out, say 'Hi, I'm Ben, what're your names?'	13 Oct	Very scary. They looked at each other and giggled. I said, 'Come on, you must have names.' I nearly got cross but it came out all right. Piers and Emily. They're twins.
At lunchtime – in the hall which is crowded and noisy and horrible.	Look for a space next someone who's sitting on their own and get talking to them. What form are you in? Have you ever had school meals or always packed lunches? Who do you think will win the world cup?	15 Oct	It was really interesting. I met this boy called Mark who only had crisps and bars and stuff. He said he wished his mum would make him sandwiches. I swapped half mine for some of his crisps. I asked him what he had to eat in the evening – frozen pizza is his favourite. He asked what happened to my nose, etc. so I told him about my cleft, also about the actor in Gladiator who has a cleft. Two of his friends came to join him and he introduced us to each other. They're in Year 8, Steve and Darren. We all talked about food. I stopped noticing how noisy and dreadful the hall is

Upon entry: *Everyone starts to look up and stare.* (*Quietly, to companions*) 'Just act natural. If anyone asks for your autograph, just sign your name.' (*To the general space*) A small, smiling bow.
Upon leaving: (*To all but not too loudly in the doorway*) 'Good night all.'

There are also situations where peers (who do not have a disfigured appearance) decide to have a laugh or have a go at the young person with the distinctive or disfigured appearance, and at their non-disfigured friend just for being with them.

Many young people with appearance anomalies have had the experience of their friends turning against them and joining the 'other side' – jeering at or ostracising them. It is unimaginably hurtful.

> Both Lizzie and Ben spoke about their experience of the few non-disabled friends they did have, suffering abuse from the larger group. Lizzie said that 'she knew she had a real friend' when that person stood up for her against the majority group.[14]

Situation 5   You've started to make some headway with one person who used to give you a hard time. But the people they used to hang out with are giving them a hard time now, for hanging out with you.

'Do you want to tough it out or shall we go and do something else?'

Situation 6   You're out with a couple of friends on your skateboards when these other kids start calling out names and stuff. You realize they're picking on your friends for choosing to be with 'Superlump'.

'I wish I knew how to stop this sort of thing. Any ideas?'

Managing difficulties in important situations

Benjamin Zephaniah met pupils in school who had done a project on his novel, *Face*, about a (white) boy making out back in school after getting burn scars in a car fire. Many of the pupils were black, and in the discussion one of them asked Benjamin if he got racist abuse and how he dealt with it.

> This is such an important question – don't we have to deal with verbal abuse most days, and it can grind a person down. It can make you want to hit out, which is never a good thing to do. Here's an example of how I deal with it myself.
>
> It's late at night, right, and I'm in London – a city I don't know well. I'm trying to find my way back to the tube station but I think I'm getting lost. There's a guy on the corner of the street, a white guy. I ask him which way to the tube station. The white guy says, 'I don't talk to blacks.' What I say to that is: I pause to steady myself, and I smile not too much, and I say, 'Man, you don't know what you're missing.' Because it's true – I wouldn't miss talking to you guys for the world.

Benjamin explained how he saw a man with a very scarred face driving the car next to his when they pulled up at red traffic lights. He found himself staring and realised that having a facial disfigurement in a world that values physical beauty could involve similar experiences he'd had to do with being black: staring, offensive comments, rude gestures . . .

Teenagers and young adults with disfigurements often report complete strangers saying to them, 'You need to see a plastic surgeon.' On the receiving end it can be hard to resist retaliating. See Chapter 5 for basic strategies for coping in these kinds of situations. But from time to time there will be a situations where it is unusually important not to let the other person carry on unchallenged or uninformed – because of who else is there, 'witnessing' the difficulty and awaiting the response to it; because the person who has got it so wrong really needs to know better (because they hold an important or influential position for instance); because what they are saying/doing is against the law.

At a close friend's party Martina, who has Moebius Syndrome, was introduced to someone she hadn't met before, who said, 'It must be so nice for you to get out and be among normal people.'

> I was among friends, many of them very good friends. It was a deep hurt right out of the blue. I was speechless – which is unusual for me! I had this image of me throwing my drink in her face. But I knew that would only make it worse – worse for my friend whose party it was, worse for me, worse for anyone else this girl ever met who looked different, worse for everyone. But I didn't want to turn the other cheek – to let her carry on regardless after being so unthinking and hurtful. Only I couldn't think how to react that would be better – that would tell her it was not okay to say this, but in a way that would do some good. What do you say at a moment like that?

> People assume there's all kinds of baggage. When I went to cast my vote, the girl behind the desk asked the person I was with, '*Would he like to vote?*' [imitating special patronizing voice she used as if talking to small child] . . . just because I *look* different.

Michelle (following one of many operations during her long recovery from 70 per cent burns to her face and body): 'I was buying a pizza and there were these lads and one of them said to me, "Why do you bother paying for it when you could just scrape it off your face with a knife?" That hurt . . . yes, that really hurt.'

Situation 7   You're buying pizza and the guy behind the counter says you're not to eat in, you have to take it out. You had been planning to eat in.

(Very calm) 'I'm sorry, what was that you just said?'
(Still calm) 'Could we just check that out with the manager? Because the Disability Discrimination Act requires you to offer me the same service as anyone else would have in here.'

Situations 8   You're at your best friend's party and someone else says something patronizing and ill-informed but possibly not unkindly meant about the way you look, such as how nice it must be for you to get out and be among normal people.

'On the contrary – how nice for *you* to have the chance to meet someone like me who can coach you on this little glitch in your social skills.'

Situations 9   You're at your best friend's party and someone else says something very rude and unkind about the way you look.

(Calm but firm) 'I think you must be confusing people's personalities with their outward appearances. I think you'll find we're both just people under our skin.'

Chapter 8

Self-perception and self-expression

Figure 8.1 Peanuts cartoon
Copyright© United Feature Syndicate, Inc. All Rights Reserved.

Looking different and being yourself

'Whenever I fell,' recalls a physically disabled girl who liked roller-skating,[1] 'out swarmed the women in droves, clucking and fretting like a bunch of bereft mother hens. It was kind of them, and in retrospect, I appreciate their solicitude, but at the time I resented and was greatly embarrassed by their interference. For they assumed that no routine hazard . . . – no stick or stone – [*tripped me*]. It was a foregone conclusion – *I fell* because I was a poor helpless cripple.'

Case study

Daisy, 6, had scars from serious burn injuries. She had spent a lot of time in hospital and was very subdued in school. Everyone who saw or met Daisy was predominantly aware of her burn scars. Her teachers struggled with her apparently unwarranted dependence on adults. 'The problem we have is she thinks she's so special. She expects special treatment. She won't take the initiative – ever. She just waits for someone else to do it.'

The children in Daisy's class were doing (fairly large) 'cut-out-people' from stiff coloured paper for a display. Folded up, only the front of the first paper person showed. Opened out, all the paper people showed. The children were writing and drawing on the paper people – their name on the first one, and all kinds of other things about themselves on the other cut-out people. Daisy was very stuck. She knew her name, and she'd been in a fire. She wore pressure garments to help her scars heal flat. She had another operation coming up in a few weeks' time. The other children, meanwhile, had loads of different things for both sides of each of their paper people. With help, Daisy was able to realize that there were more things she could add – things she could do and things she enjoyed – but it took a long time (see Figure 8.2). When all the paper people were threaded up and displayed in the classroom, Daisy noticed that some of the children had written and drawn things similar to her own. The other children were able to discover new things about Daisy, including things that they had in common with her.

When the display came down, Daisy kept her paper Daisy in her tray. She added more paper people on the end, to write and draw about the new things she'd done and the things the teacher had noticed about her.

She talked and listened more. Sometimes she was seen holding her paper Daisy, folded flat, in a tight hug against her body. She became more willing to 'have a go'.

An early years centre with a number of children who had disabilities including disfigurement created a 'passport' for each child. In photographs and words, the passport recorded and communicated a range of child-centred information – the things the child wanted to say about themselves such as '*What I enjoy*', '*My family and home*', information another professional might need to know, answers to the kinds of questions often asked by other children or their parents . . . A girl with mobility issues used her passport to say that she used a wheelchair but that she could crawl and pull herself up to the table or onto a chair. *If I need your help I will ask you*.[2]

In the ordinary run of things, the way we 'see' ourselves, the things we know about ourselves, is something that just happens. However, it is not always a straightforward process. Children and young people with low self-esteem (which includes many pupils with facial disfigurement) can find it hard to take in anything positive about themselves (see Chapter 6). As well as their outward appearance being excessively noticeable (and their inner qualities thereby overshadowed) young children with injuries and conditions that affect the way they look may have fewer experiences to help them develop a broad and positive self-perception. Medical treatment can entail long periods of physical restriction. Their contact with peers may be curtailed. They may be kept at home to avoid the

Figure 8.2 Daisy's 'cut-out people'. Daisy needed a clearer sense of her inner qualities to balance her noticeable appearance (see case study)

problem of other people's reactions, or they may be withdrawn or angry in response to these reactions. Any or all of these can give rise to a limited or skewed self-perception.

Opportunities to do more and different things, alone and with others, enable children to develop a better sense of their abilities, preferences and other personal qualities. It is also important to have these attributes and experiences accurately recognized and named.

Pupil or patient?

School is an important part of a child's world. Learning and play, time in lessons and time with other children, daily journeys between school and home, are what being a child is all about. Being a patient, particularly in the early stages after surgery or a traumatic injury, could not be more different from school. It lasts all night as well as all day. Parents are worried and the whole family routine is disrupted for days or weeks. The ward is primarily an adult world and a medical world. There may be a great deal of pain and fear. Sessions with a play specialist or a teacher from the hospital school are scheduled when there is time between medical events. There are usually a few other children, but they are also in various stages of treatment and recovery.

> Ryan had another operation in Year 5 and his class teacher was wonderful. They all sent him get well soon cards – which he still has, aged 14. It made a huge difference, this feeling that they were thinking of him, rooting for him.

> Maneesh was away nearly the whole term. It was too far to visit but the hospital had a school and I arranged with a teacher there to send him some of the work he was missing. He didn't do much but the teacher said he liked to have it. We also sent him a tape recording of several of his classmates telling jokes and we did birthday cards when he turned 9. I spoke with him by phone a couple of times. Looking back, I think we should have tried to set that up so that he could have a chat with his friends instead of his teacher.

For children and young people who have good peer relations at school, a hospital stay can make them feel very 'out of it'. For children who mix less easily at school, a hospital stay can reinforce social skills skewed towards the company of adults, the attentions of medical specialists. Maintaining a child or young person's sense of belonging at school can be of enormous importance while they are away in hospital. Managing their transition back into school afterwards is also important.

> When Nina came back after half term, she seemed to have gone backwards. Before, she'd learnt to do quite a few things for herself, getting what she needed from her tray, buttoning her coat, choosing a book . . . I couldn't *believe* she wasn't just having me on, standing there waiting for someone else to take her in hand.

> While I was away, my year went on a trip to the science museum. I really wanted to go. My dad said we'd go in the holidays but that isn't the same. Afterwards the teacher gave me some of the photos and I did a project called *The trip I missed*. I did go in the summer and put some more bits in the project, about atmosphere and why the sky's blue and stuff. But my favourite photo was the one of everyone having their picnic by the Thames – in the rain!

Falling behind with school-work can be a serious worry for pupils, particularly as they get older. Careful thought and sensible, focused decisions about what to catch up on and what to omit are essential. A pupil with a realistic programme of work and achievable targets will do better than a pupil who feels swamped or left behind.

Getting different messages

At home, among family and friends, as well as in hospital, a child may receive responses and feedback from adults which differ in subtle but important ways from the kind of interactions children experience who are not visibly different.

'[M]others of atypical infants often demonstrate . . . poorly organized play, stereotypic and fixed facial expressions . . . interrupted feedings . . . and often over-stimulate their infants'. They were also more directive, less responsive to social behaviours from their children, and provided more poorly differentiated consequences to compliant and non-compliant behaviours than did mothers of 'normal' children at similar developmental levels.[2]

Observed in a large coffee shop:

> A number of young mothers with their very young children were reorganizing the tables to make room for several highchairs. It was just before Christmas – a special outing for them all. More of the party arrived until there were eight or nine mothers and about a dozen infants from new-borns to toddlers. Most of the children were of a similar age – perhaps it was an ante-natal class that had bonded particularly well a couple of years ago. One of the little ones, with his or her back to me, was vaguely noticeable – there was something about the shape of the back of the head, a bit flat maybe.
>
> He or she seemed alert but quiet. So you hardly noticed anything different from the back – in fact what you noticed was the way each mother in turn interacted with this infant compared with all the others. It was like they just over-did it. Well-intentioned but too much coochycoochycoo, too loud – almost like it was more for others to see, or they were reassuring themselves that this child was okay. Somehow it just wasn't something mutual between themselves and the child. Then when they moved the high-chair to fit another couple of mums into the group, you saw the little one did look rather different – head sort of long from top to bottom and flat from front to back, lower part of face rather large, eyes rather small, tongue inclined to be out. Not so conventionally cute-looking as the others – different-looking.

The attention shown towards, or withheld from, small children who look different can lead, in time, to acute self-consciousness and feelings of conspicuousness (see p. 43). A child or young person who has become routinely nervous and hesitant may keep their eyes averted or downward-looking. Avoiding other people's faces in order to avoid the experience of being looked at or stared at has the additional effect of avoiding perceiving whatever the other person's appearance conveys. In fact body language and facial expression convey a great deal and often convey more than spoken words. Most people can recognize anger, fear, happiness and sadness from posture alone.[4]

A pupil's reluctance to look at other people – though understandable – effectively deprives them of a whole swathe of important information about what's going on around them and how others are relating to them. They will need guidance and practice in order to make a conscious effort to notice how other people look and act – and *feel*.

Giving positive and accurate non-verbal messages

A young person who makes more eye-contact in order to know more about what's going on will gain the bonus of appearing physically more at ease. Curiously, an improved feeling of well-being is apt to arise within the person who is adopting a more open, confident-looking body posture.

This in turn can open the way for a pupil to benefit from developing a broader repertoire of non-verbal communication. Since we all gather so much information by looking at each other's faces, this can be important for a child or young person whose speech is affected. However, scarring, cranio-facial differences and other unusual facial features can significantly affect this aspect of communication in various ways:

- as already mentioned, by a tendency to avoid eye-contact
- because the condition or injury (scarring for instance) restricts the subtle facial movements which give 'expression'
- previous experience of being told to 'be brave' during painful medical procedures, or to 'ignore it' when being taunted by others may have taught the child not to show any feelings
- a desire to avoid being noticed may lead a young person to develop a form of self-effacement which includes minimizing facial expression.

Observing the child in a range of situations, with both peers and adults, is an important first step. How much does their non-verbal communication contribute to others' awareness of what they are feeling and thinking?

> Kate had this way of suddenly running off a few paces, hugging herself, with her head tilted hard over to one side. For a long time we couldn't make it out. Someone had to step back and watch – not the teacher, they'd be too involved, too much going on. Eventually it began to seem like Kate did this when she actually *liked* what was going on – when she was feeling keen or happy or excited – like these feelings would get a bit overwhelming or something. What I imagine is that this reaction had come out of being banned from grabbing you in a huggy way – maybe she'd been told off a lot for that. Now she's learning to do thumbs up and a little bit of running on the spot – it's much less confusing for everyone else.

If a child or young person's non-verbal expressions have become shaped in ways which are hard for others to interpret, it can be very helpful for them to explore new ways of identifying and expressing their feelings. This may not be a simple or straightforward task but require considerable time, skill and patience. A child who has learnt to avoid looking at others and possibly also to block off their own uncomfortable or unhappy feelings may have to start from scratch:

1 noticing how others look and act in order to identify what they are feeling and thinking
2 noticing how they themselves are feeling in certain specific and defined situations
3 identifying and naming different feelings
4 expressing feelings non-verbally – body language, gesture.

Table 8.1 Showing how you feel

Situation . . .	. . . makes you feel . . .	. . . how to show this	How am I doing?
Getting picked for the mini-bus trip you really wanted to go on	Happy, triumphant	Nice fists palms forward arms up	Too much – don't jump up
Getting sponsors for walk	Determined	Fist into flat palm	Hold it still for a few moments
Maths test	Nervous, reluctant	Fluttering fingers, hand pushing away	Good
Exam results – better than expected	Relieved	Hand on chest, big sigh	Good
Dead fly in cake	Disgusted	Hand grips throat	
Bump into corner of desk	Hurt (physical)	Rub hurting place	
Called names	Hurt (inside)	Self-hug	
Being blamed – not my fault	Angry, unfair	Jerk fist, jerk head	
Miss the bus	Frustrated, annoyed	Slam fists against hips	
Out with dog on sunny, windy day	Very happy	Tall, wide	
Heard this joke before	Bored	Sagging all over	

Verbal expression

As mentioned above, some people may have their scope for facial expression severely restricted or simply not present at all (because of extensive burns to the face, or facial paralysis, or Moebius, for instance). As well as expression through body-language and gesture, it will be important for this pupil to develop good powers of verbal expression – a fifth stage in the process of acquiring good, accurate self-expressions.

5   putting feelings into words

Vocabulary, emphasis, pitch, tone and volume are all very important.

Self-presentation

Other aspects of self-presentation have important social effects too. However, drawing pupils' attention to the 'image' represented by clothes, the manner in which they are worn, and other aspects of physical attitude, can seem like the wrong thing to do. Particularly in the context of disfigurement, people's 'inner qualities' are more important – surely? And doesn't paying more attention to issues of style and fashion risk contributing to eating disorders? Certainly, sensitivity is required.

School uniform can be both helpful and unhelpful. It can smooth over problems of self-presentation, during school at least. But it can also hide difficulties which a child may be having in this area.

A counsellor recalls:

> Previously Sue had come in school uniform but as it was half term she came in jeans. I'd never realized what a tough-looking tomboy she was. It did leave me wondering whether she really does want to get in with the girls in her class. Would she be happy doing each other's hair, painting nails, trying on each other's skimpy tops? Sue looked more like she'd like to scrape barnacles off an old boat and set off for a seriously big adventure. Or at least play a lot of football in the park.

A non-stereotypical self-presentation may be seen as antisocial. Physical conformity and peer similarity are associated with popularity and friendship selection.[5] The messages conveyed by clothes, shoes, hair, jewellery and hand-luggage can be profound and very subtle. The kind of neat-and-tidy appearance which pleases adults may be totally naff among peers. At the very least, children and young people need an opportunity to check out whether they want to join in this style thing, and if so, the do's and don'ts – the 'dress code' – for conveying what they'd like to convey. Discussions involving peers are likely to be more useful and accurate than talking with adults!

Chapter 9

Looking anew at a pupil's situation

Most help . . . assumes that the problem lies within the child and tries to 'cure' it. But a growing number of professionals feel that problems within an individual are merely reflections of difficulties within a family or school, or even more broadly, a reflection of the problems or evils of society itself.[1]

Andrew

The nursery leader was concerned about the difficult, sometimes unmanageable behaviour of a 3-year-old boy with a cleft lip and palate. Sometimes he would 'lash out' at other children. At home-time he sometimes ran wild. The leader contacted *Changing Faces* for advice. Two quite involved telephone calls followed, initially exploring the possibility that Andrew might be having difficulty in identifying and expressing his own feelings and preferences and in 'reading' other people's. (This sometimes seems to be problematic, and may be linked to the research finding that mothers of children with disfigurements tend to look at them less when they are playing. See p. 67)

The nursery leader also arranged for *Changing Faces* to contact Andrew's mother, and the speech therapist at a specialist nursery for children with delayed speech which he was also attending, part-time. It soon emerged that the boy's mother also had a cleft – she had previously had contact with *Changing Faces* on her own behalf some years earlier (before she had Andrew) and had found this helpful. Through further telephone counselling sessions, Andrew's mother (who had an older child without a cleft) was able to explore the negative feelings she had felt towards her son since an early scan revealed that he would be born with a cleft. She described her own childhood as having been 'hell both at home and at school', on account of her cleft.

This counselling process made it easier for the mother to see Andrew separately from herself, to pay him more attention, and, with the help of a local course for parenting skills, Andrew began to relax and settle down.

Ryan

Before Ryan started school, the staff found out, with his mother Gill's help, everything they thought they needed to know about Ryan's cleft lip and palate.

> I wanted him to fit in and be treated just like all the other children. Then one day the teacher said to me, 'Do you know why Ryan doesn't want to do any painting

or messy play in the water or sand-tray?' I was puzzled as he was always painting at home or messing about with a bowl of playdough. I gave it some thought and gently queried this with Ryan. But at just turned 4 years old, he offered no explanation.

I offered to go into to school to help out as a 'parent helper'. There, it hit me – the painting aprons were just like 'hospital gowns'. No wonder he wouldn't want to paint. But why didn't he want to play in the sand and water? They didn't have to wear aprons here! Then I heard the teacher asking the children to pull up their sleeves in order not to get them wet or messy. What happens nearly every time Ryan visits hospital? Blood samples or injections. Ryan would always struggle to hang on to his sleeves at this point. He obviously needed to be reassured that these new surroundings were pain-free![2]

Hannah

Hannah's mother was disturbed by her able and independent daughter's change in attitude soon after starting secondary school. Where before she'd been an enthusiastic pupil who was keen to get on with her homework in the evenings, now she was grumpier and more reluctant each morning and only opened her bag to do her homework after a great deal of chivvying. Even more worrying, Hannah's eczema was deteriorating after a long period of settled improvement.

Friends? Yes. Bullying? No. Was the work too hard? No. Were the teachers nice? Y-y-yes.

At half-term, Hannah's mother noticed that the tub of emollient which Hannah carried in her school-bag to re-cream her sore places was nowhere near as used-up as it should have been after six or seven weeks at school. It emerged that Hannah had been severely reprimanded for arriving late, three weeks running, to the maths lesson which followed PE. 'Once more and I'll have you moved down to set two.' She had also been told off for arriving late to registration after the lunchtime gymnastics club which she had therefore given up. Day after day she'd struggled to choose between creaming to keep her eczema under control and getting to lessons on time.

At a meeting with the class teacher it was agreed that Hannah *and a friend* would leave PE early so that they would be in time for Maths. In order to go to lunchtime gymnastics, Hannah *and a friend* were excused afternoon registration that day, so long as they reminded the form teacher on the relevant morning that this was what would be happening. The maths teacher (whose telling off might have been easier to shrug off if Hannah had disliked him or disliked maths!) apologized for having jumped to the wrong conclusion without asking any questions.

Tom

Tom was having a hard time at school. How were the other children to be stopped from calling him 'Fat cheek'? After a detailed discussion with the School Specialist at *Changing Faces*, action was taken. Here is Tom's mother's account of his special assembly for Years 3 and 4:

It started off with an introduction from a teacher, talking in general terms about how we all look different and although some people may look a little more different than others we all have the same feelings and emotions underneath. It was stressed that it was usually okay to ask sensible questions about someone's appearance but that it was not at all acceptable to tease or bully a person because of the way they look.

Then Tom went up to the front and gave a brief talk about cystic hygroma and how it affects him. The children all listened very attentively and their understanding was definitely helped by the teacher reiterating each section of Tom's speech to them.

When Tom invited questions a sea of hands shot up. He coped very well with answering most of the questions, needing just a little help from the teacher and me. The session extended into playtime with a handful of children staying behind to ask Tom even more questions. The most amazing thing was that several children came up to Tom, unprompted, at the end of the assembly and publicly apologized to him.

The individual classes are going to follow up the assembly with classroom discussions and reading *Showtime*. I also prepared an information sheet about Tom which has been distributed to all staff at the school and have had a meeting with the headteacher to discuss the school's policies for teasing and bullying, strategies for Tom to deal with any problems and also ways in which the school could help Tom to build up his self-esteem and confidence in social situations. I am delighted with the way the school is supporting us.

Here is the speech Tom prepared for his Year 3 and 4 assembly[3]:
My face looks different from other people because I have got something called cystic hygroma. Not many people have heard of cystic hygroma or know what it is. When I was younger and didn't know much about it, I used to think it made me clever! I decided to find out about cystic hygroma and this is what I learned.

Most people know that blood is carried around our bodies in vessels or tubes. There is also another type of fluid called lymph, which goes around our bodies in tubes called lymphatic vessels. My cystic hygroma is caused by lots of little cysts or bumps on the lymphatic vessels in my cheek.

Cystic hygroma is very rare. There are probably less than 1,000 children in the whole of the country who have it. So if I were a Pokémon* card I would probably be worth a lot of money!

My cystic hygroma is quite difficult to treat. When I was 4 I went into hospital to have an operation that made my cheek a little bit smaller. I missed two weeks of school but it wasn't much fun because my face felt quite sore for a long time afterwards. At the moment I have to go to hospital every three or four months. I have to breathe in sleeping gas through a special mask and then, while I am asleep, the doctor injects a drug into my cheek. The drug is called OK-432 and we hope it will make my cheek smaller.

I also went to hospital to have an ultrasound scan on my cheek. It was a bit like having an x-ray but instead of looking at my bones, I could see the inside of my face on a screen. Sometimes people tease me or say unkind things about my face. Cystic hygroma doesn't make me any different inside from other people, it's just something you're born with like the colour of your eyes, whether you have freckles or moles, whether your hair is straight or curly, and so on.

If anyone has got any questions that they would like to ask me, I'll have a go at answering them . . .

* Collecting and trading Pokémon cards was a popular hobby at this time and the goal of a complete set made rarer cards very sought-after.

Following a session like 'Tom's assembly', it is important that teachers – resourced with some background information about appearance and disfigurement – run classroom discussions:

1   *Showtime* can be used to reassure pupils that it is all right to feel curious and to ask questions, and that being 'different' can be interesting and impressive.
2   'Who's been in hospital? What was it like? Who's had an injection? What's it like being given sleeping gas to breathe?' Most children will have had at least one experience of this kind. They may have cried at the time and parents felt it best not to raise it in conversation afterwards. But a hospital visit, an injection, some time off school, may give a child an important shared experience with a classmate who, on the face of it, seems merely 'different'.
3   'Has anyone ever had that horrible feeling of being "the odd one out"?' Children need to explore feeling noticeable or self-conscious – after getting a pair of glasses, for instance, or having a radical hair-cut, or wearing the wrong clothes to a party.
4   'Have you ever been somewhere and there was someone – or a group of other people – who looked different and you got told not to stare?'

There were all these people – grown-ups – in the swimming pool. Maybe six or eight of them. You could see they were . . . like . . . disabled or something. Some of them used this lift thing to get down into the water. Each one had a helper to do the swimming. Except one, this lady, she was a good swimmer with just one arm. She had two arms but she only used one. The arm she didn't use had an inflated arm-band round, maybe just to help keep that side from sinking down or something. I knew it was wrong to stare, but I was *interested*. Someone told me they all go to some Day Centre place and swimming would be like a treat, like maybe it was someone's birthday or something. Afterwards, when I was telling my Mum, I realized I wouldn't mind a job helping people go swimming like that. It was . . . cool.

Luke

Luke was a Year 9 pupil with a very noticeable facial disfigurement, whose poor performance across the curriculum and whose behaviour (especially verbal fights with peers – 'cussing') were causing serious concern.

Luke had a Statement of Special Educational Needs because his sight had been affected by his facial disfigurement. There was talk of a re-assessment in case he needed to attend a school for pupils with learning difficulties. His parents arranged for an educational psychologist to assess their son (privately). His intelligence, and in particular his reading age, were well above average.

During a meeting with Luke's teachers, a very concerned member of staff asked the *Changing Faces* School Specialist, 'How long is he expected to live?' It emerged that the parents had asked for nothing to be said at all about Luke's condition, so that he could be treated 'just like everyone else' at school. No-one knew what made his face and head look as they did – it was easy to imagine a cancerous tumour.

Staff were provided with factual information about Luke's disfiguring condition and details of his above average scores in the educational psychologist's assessment. They were also told about 'high achieving' career-minded adults who happen to have this condition.

In addition to extra support in some lessons because of sight/fine motor skills difficulties, the LEA funded one-to-one counselling for the pupil. The counselling was, of course, confidential, but in due course a request emerged for Luke's tutor group – who'd been with him since Year 7 with only his distinctive appearance and his relentless 'cussing' to go on – to be told about his disfiguring condition. Luke did not want to do this himself.

However, he participated fully in the preparations for a series of three lessons. (1) Pupils imagine acquiring an injury or condition which affected the way they look and explore how their friends, and strangers, would react to them (*Face* by Bejamin Zephaniah can be a good way into this). (2) A lesson uses *Changing Faces* resources on the social psychology of appearance and disfigurement. (3) Pupils create posters and informations leaflets to inform and persuade others regarding visible difference. The lessons were geared to promoting knowledge *and empathy* about living with a disfiguring injury or condition and were run without any reference whatsoever to Luke. It was left to Luke himself to decide whether or not to attend the lessons.

The final task for pupils was to create an information leaflet or wall-poster for pupils in other tutor groups who had not had the 'talk' – to use their newly acquired 'expertise' to promote positive attitudes to difference.

Over the ensuing months Luke's attitude to schoolwork gradually altered. From having been thought to be in need of a place at a special school for people with learning difficulties, he was expected to gain A-C grades at GCSE. (He continued to relate to peers largely through the medium of 'cussing' and it was not till he transferred to a sixth form college that his interactions with peers became more conventionally 'friendly'.)

Kylie

When Kylie was 13 years old it was noticed that one of her shoulders was higher than the other, and she could not seem to put this right by 'standing straight'. Also at this time, a close school friend died of cancer. She became reluctant to go to school. GCSE subject choices had separated her from her friends. She complained of staring and name-calling.

The head of year was approached and action was taken to identify and punish the name-callers. Kylie's timetable was altered so that she attended lessons with her familiar group of friends again.

Still she did not want to go to school. It was arranged for friends to call for her on the way to school so that she would not have to go into the building on her own. But even this did not reduce her reluctance. The Education Welfare Officer became involved. Kylie continued to complain of feeling unbearably self-conscious, and of staring and name-calling.

Kylie told the *Changing Faces* psychologist about being diagnosed with a scoliosis – a deformity, the hospital specialist had explained, which she'd had since birth. Kylie was offered cranio-facial surgery to improve the slight facial asymmetry which this condition emphasized.

The *Changing Faces* psychologist continued to help her develop strategies for dealing with feelings of self-consciousness. They also worked on increasing her range of responses when people called her names. (She mostly tried to ignore them but often shouted back before walking away.) Still she could hardly bear to leave the house.

The planned surgery was 'fast-tracked' because of worries about Kylie's schoolwork. Meanwhile, a further approach was made to the head of year to try and improve things at school. He replied that Kylie's facial asymmetry was so slight that most people didn't notice it. The school friends she had been reunited with were also very poor attenders. Her form tutor was relatively new and had 'not got to grips with' the form yet. Pupils who were apt to tease had been told not to, again.

Kylie did not return to school before the surgery. After ten days in hospital she seemed pleased with her altered appearance. But still, nothing seemed to make it any easier for her to return to school. Her GCSE work was falling far behind.

Her GP referred her to a clinical psychologist. Confidentiality limits what can be known about this, but after a few sessions the psychologist wrote to the school: Kylie was overwhelmed by the backlog of GCSE work – could something be done to make this more manageable and support her with it? Kylie was especially sensitive to people sitting behind her – could lessons be arranged so that she could find somewhere to sit where she felt less vulnerable? She had been particularly embarrassed by walking into the wrong classroom where everyone stared and laughed before she backed out and closed the door – could she have some help with knowing where she was meant to be and finding her way around? She found class groups most difficult when she did not know the other people – she needed to know what to expect – which lessons had familiar people in and which ones had people in who were new to her.

The EWO developed a part-time school timetable, with part-time attendance at a nearby facility based in an ordinary house. Also, some work experience was set up. Kylie continued to work on strategies for dealing with staring, curiosity, and teasing. Things gradually improved.

A small breakthrough came on work experience when a colleague (an adult) asked about her uneven shoulders. Kylie 'heard herself laugh' as she gave one of the answers she had been practising.

In due course, although Kylie's GCSEs were not all they might have been, she reached the end of Year 11 with her social confidence somewhat restored, with the skills she needed to meet new people and with a positive attitude to both work and further education.

What can we infer from these case studies?

Information not answers   A 'problem' with a pupil is like a jigsaw puzzle which has become scattered. Information, like pieces, must be gathered from every possible place. There will be pieces that don't help much and pieces that are hard to place. The puzzle can be damaged by trying to force a piece that looks as if it must fit. There may be pieces from some other puzzle, mixed in by mistake. Puzzles take time and patience, but gradually a sense of the picture begins to emerge.

Take unhappiness, fear and distress very seriously   You go into the wrong room and everyone laughs . . . How safe and secure should a pupil expect to feel at school?

Special listening   A pupil with a disfiguring injury or condition may never see or meet anyone else who looks like them, or who's been through what they've been through. Their sense of isolation can make it almost impossible to find the words to share an experience or a feeling with anyone else. It requires someone to listen with openness, empathy and imagination.

A one-to-one counsellor, or a trained member of staff who is enabled (allowed the time) simply to listen, may address the special educational needs of a pupil with a disfigurement in the same way that ramps and automatic doors can meet the mobility needs of a pupil in a wheelchair.

Network as safety net   Open channels of communication between family, school, medical services and other agencies are hugely important.

Pupil-centred solutions   If a pupil can muster the courage to talk directly to their peers, combined with opportunities for all pupils to reflect upon their own experiences, this works better than a member of staff 'giving a talk' (see pp. 36 and 87). If the pupil does not feel ready for this, a 'role model' with a similar condition and similar experiences is the next best solution. Keep the information-sharing direct and personal and involve all pupils – never talk to a group of pupils about a pupil or let the injury or condition become the main subject matter.

Empower school staff   School staff will need information and training about appearance and disfigurement, to enable them to prepare and run lessons and manage social interactions which adequately take account of the social psychology of visible difference.

Talking not outlawing   A carefully managed discussion about what people may think or feel – questions, anecdotes, personal responses – is often more effective than reiterating that teasing and bullying are wrong (see Chapter 5).

Has it worked?   Keep monitoring the situation carefully afterwards. Sometimes improvements last, sometimes they don't. Be prepared to try other approaches (look for more pieces of the jigsaw puzzle).

Chapter 10

Thinking about careers

When a pupil or student with a disfigurement is considering their future, there may be particular concerns. Are there some jobs, careers or working environments that are just not suitable for a person with a disfigurement? How will they cope with meeting a lot of new people, on work experience, or later when they go to college?

What follows here is not a careers programme, but pointers for each stage of the pupil's progress through the ordinary school careers curriculum:

- identifying and recording personal qualities
- career ideas – adults may choose work where they have little contact with the general public and children are given less opportunities in school to show their real abilities.[1] What do we mean by 'realistic'?
- work experience – using public transport and meeting new people call for special preparation, monitoring and following up
- applying for jobs and courses – form-filling and writing a CV – 'Is it best to mention my difference?'
- selection interviews and overcoming employer bias against recruiting 'people with problems'
- anti-discrimination legislation.

Identifying and recording personal qualities

For a pupil who has a visible difference it is especially important for their Achievement File (or equivalent) to include:

- a full, accurate and up-to-date record of skills, abilities and aptitudes, experiences and achievements, interests and preferences (see Chapter 8)
- a photographic record – *action shots* – of achievements which show the pupil as well as what they've been doing. It is better if disfigurements of face or hands, for instance, are not 'taboo' subjects but are just a part of the whole picture
- information about absences from school for medical treatment, balanced by the way they have learnt to deal with this: working independently, prioritizing, being well-organized
- social experiences, activities and achievements as part of a group
- positive aspects of their injury or condition, such as experiences they might not otherwise have had, or people they would not otherwise have met

- experiences and achievements which are quite unconnected to their appearance or the injury or condition that has affected them.

Career ideas

Most adults are sceptical when a child says s/he wants to become an astronaut. But some men and women are astronauts. What, then, if a young person with a facial disfigurement wants to work in film?

> I was always interested in literature and drama and I wanted to work in theatre. But I found school hard because of teasing and bullying. Teachers and the careers officer were very dismissive. So I had to sort of figure it out for myself. The college took me without the right GCSEs – they liked what I said at interview I suppose. I started out doing photography and it was really hard, socially, at first. But the lecturers were supportive and helped me recognize my strengths. The other students were great too, once we'd got to know each other. Now I'm on a degree course in animation.

Some injuries and conditions do pose a particular challenge in certain environments and may affect specific activities. Particularly if the hands are affected, skin conditions such as eczema or psoriasis, or scars in the process of healing, can make it difficult for people to sustain tasks which involve water, chemicals, grit or heat (including the wearing of nylon overalls) and can also significantly reduce dexterity.

The important thing for any pupil is to *find out more* about any career they might be interested in. What is day-to-day life like for a person in this line of work? What are the personal qualities that go best with this job? What is the down-side? What about academic requirements, training and opportunities? Good careers information is essential. If not available in school, the local careers office or youth advisory service can usually offer interactive software and other services for exploring careers in detail alongside personal qualities, abilities and preferences.

Work experience

It may be tempting to arrange a 'sheltered' placement to minimize travelling or encountering new people. But something more open, well-prepared and well-monitored will do more to help the pupil prepare to leave school positively.

During Kylie's difficult journey out of non-attendance and back towards the main stream a small breakthrough came on work experience when a colleague (an adult) asked about her uneven shoulders – and Kylie 'heard herself laugh' as she gave one of the answers she had been learning (see p. 90).

Preparation

Especially if 'nobody notices' the pupil's difference at school any more, ensure that they have at least one effective strategy for dealing with other people's reactions – staring, curiosity, concern, or just uneasiness (see Chapter 2). If not, this should be tackled as a priority.

Would they like the people at the place of work where they will be spending their two or three weeks to have some information beforehand about their disfigurement? This is usually done by asking the boss to say something about it to everyone they will be working with. The pupil will need to decide what they want the boss to say.

> Jo will be here next week, on work experience from the high school. She's had an operation which has left a bit of a scar on her face, but it's no problem. If you find yourself staring just smile and say Hi. At the moment she's thinking about a career in accounts, so I guess she'll be interested in how our systems work and the spreadsheets we use and so on.

The people at the place of work may be uncertain about how to 'make it all right' for a pupil on work experience who has a disfigured appearance.

> The office manager asked anxiously, 'Is there anything we can do to help it go well for you?' The pupil with severe facial disfigurement thought for a moment. Then, 'Yes, perhaps there is.' He suddenly grinned. 'Pay me!'

The most useful preliminary advice may be – as Jo did in her suggestion to her work-experience boss, above – to reassure people about staring rather than telling them not to stare. (They will probably be telling themselves not to stare anyway – which could result in the pupil feeling ignored and isolated.)

'If you find yourself staring, smile and say Hi.'
'If you find yourself focusing on my mouth, try and make eye-contact instead.'
'If you're curious and want to ask a question, I don't usually mind – but be prepared to tell me something about yourself too.'

Encourage all pupils to record in their work experience diary or log some notes about managing an unfamiliar journey and meeting new people. Specific examples of things that went well and things that didn't go so well are especially useful.

Monitoring

Monitoring needs to be done sooner rather than later so that any misunderstandings about staring or other social difficulties can be addressed straight away. As well as all the usual checks about attendance and performance at their work tasks, the member of staff carrying out the monitoring needs to *ask and observe* how the pupil is getting on with the (new) people they are working with. A checklist should include:

- greeting people/responding to greetings upon arrival each day
- learning and using people's names
- contributions/responses during conversations at tea-breaks/lunchtime
- if speech is affected, ability to involve others in supplementary/alternative modes of communication.

Clear notes with specific examples are vital for de-briefing later!

Afterwards the whole experience can be seen as a 'dry run' for the bigger step of leaving school to go to college or to start a job or a training course (see Table 10.1).

Table 10.1 Work experience review – looking ahead

	How did it go this time?			Changes worth considering for next time
	Best thing	*Worst thing*	*General comments*	
The work itself				
The working environment				
Relations with supervisor(s)				
Getting on with other people on the job				
Meeting others during breaks, etc.				
Journey to and from place of work				
If staff were 'prepared' for visible difference . . .				
If staring, curiosity, etc. was dealt with (or not) using 'having something to say' . . .				

Applying for courses and jobs

Targeting

Encourage the pupil to keep rejections to a minimum by running a few checks before applying.

(A) Qualifications, personal attributes, etc. as in job specification or course details	*(B) Qualifications, personal attributes, relevant experience, etc. to go on CV or application form*
List them all . . .	List them all . . . A well maintained, up-to-date progress file is invaluable for this.

If the A-list and B-list aren't a good match, the pupil may want to consider rejecting the opportunity as unsuitable. If they remain keen, can they compensate for the mismatch in a covering letter?

> My lack of hands-on experience of fish farming is more than made up for by all the fishing I have done and all the books and angling magazines I've read since I was 11 years old.

Alternatively, a pupil may decide to apply for several different courses or a wide range of different jobs. CVs can be sent speculatively to several firms who may have work or training that interests them, without a strong sense of commitment to any particular one, but just to see 'what comes up'. This is a perfectly valid approach, but it does increase the risk of rejections and of getting no reply.

'Is it best to mention my difference?'

Application forms often have a section inviting candidates to give any further information which they think might be relevant. A CV just needs an extra heading for this extra information. Alternatively, a brief accompanying letter can be used to say something about the pupil's disfigurement, *if they think it is in their interest to do so*. This is a tough decision to make.

Good reasons to say something might be:

- to demonstrate that they have an advantage over other candidates. For example, 'I have a large birthmark on the left side of my face. Because of my unusual appearance, I have learned how to take the initiative in social situations and put people at ease. I think the social skills that I have developed make me very good at dealing with the public and, in combination with the qualifications, experience and interests listed elsewhere on this form, I feel that I am an ideal candidate for this job.'
- to inform people so that they do not react with undue surprise and awkwardness at the interview. For example, 'I have a condition called Moebius Syndrome which means I have no movement in my face. Some people find this disconcerting when they first meet me, such as at a job interview, but they soon get used to me as they get to know me. My facial condition is not a problem to me and, as you can see from my answers to the other questions on this form, I have the right interests and experience for this job and am set to achieve good qualifications in the summer.'

A pupil may, of course, prefer not to mention their appearance at this stage. The obvious argument for this is that it prevents an employer from acting on prejudice or worrying about 'the unknown' and deciding not to interview.

Ultimately each individual must judge whether they are more comfortable when meeting people who have been prepared in some way for their different appearance, or whether they prefer to tackle things face to face at the first meeting.

Interviews

Arrange for at least one 'mock interview' with someone not known to the pupil. A local employer's forum (e.g. Round Table) or college can often provide someone to help with this. Or schools can come to a reciprocal arrangement where staff provide mock interviews for each other's pupils.

The interviewer needs:

- information about the course or job the pupil is going for (in some detail if outside their usual field)

- a mocked-up or photocopied application form, including something about the pupil's appearance if they have decided to say something in advance
- a checklist of the kind of feedback required:
  - arrival/entering room/greeting
  - eye contact, speaking voice, body language, manner
  - answers to questions.

Beforehand

Even if the interviewer has already been informed about the candidate's disfigurement, the pupil should prepare for the possibility that someone who hasn't met them before will tend to focus on their disfigurement and may not get a full picture of the person they really are. See Chapter 2, *Having something to say*.

Shaking hands

If the hands are affected, it is particularly important to say something before or during the handshake. 'As you can see, my skin has been quite badly affected by psoriasis. Which isn't catching, by the way – it's just a condition that makes the skin very dry. I've never let it hold me back at school, and it won't hold me back at college either.'

A young man who was partially deaf and also had a serious skin condition commented, 'When I went into the hearing support unit, the staff there shook my hand and smiled and welcomed me. I'll never forget it. It was the first time anyone had ever shaken hands with me without, like, recoiling from the way my skin is.'

Even if the hands are not affected, handshakes are worth practising – the aim is to make eye contact and say hello during the handshake, rather than looking at the hands!

Be prepared

Anticipate the interviewer's possible (or probable) doubts or assumptions about the suitability of a person who 'looks different' by preparing things to say, especially *examples*, to overcome these concerns.

- *Disfigurement is an illness and this candidate will take lot of time off sick.* If there has been surgery or other treatment involving time off school, say so – especially if exam achievements may have been affected. But also find somewhere in the interview to mention good attendance (if school attendance has been good!).
- *Anyone who looks different will want to work behind the scenes.* If this is the pupil's preference, they should make a positive statement about this such as, 'In school, I did a lot of work in the library, putting books away, keeping all the records in order, sending out reminders. People outside don't notice that kind of work but it's what makes the place run smoothly.' If the pupil prefers a more visible role, they must ensure the interviewer knows this. 'I'm good at meeting new people and putting them at their ease. At school I am often picked to show visitors round and it's something that I enjoy doing. I think it's important not to appear nervous even when that's a bit how you're feeling.'

- *Anyone who looks like this must be lonely and depressed.* Tone and body language will be the main tools here (see Chapter 8, *Self-perception and self-expression.*) 'My friends don't even notice my scars any more – we just get on with having a good time and stuff. New people are sometimes surprised because of how I look, so I've learnt to say Hi and try to put them at ease.'
- *Looking like this means 'special needs' – if they came here we'd have to change everything to accommodate them.* The pupil's relevant experience (Saturday job, spare time interest, school project, etc.) can be reassuring. 'The best thing we did in school was the French teacher took us cycling in northern France, all along the coast, staying at youth hostels and cycling about 50 kilometres each day. It was brilliant.' Or, 'I'm very calm and patient when there's something tricky and involved to be done. I had a lot of plastic surgery when I was younger, after I got burnt in a house-fire. It takes a long time but it teaches you about doing things properly, attention to detail, not making a fuss.'

A presentation folder or progress file can be used to shift the interviewer's attention away from the candidate's unusual appearance and towards their achievements and capabilities as a potential recruit. This requires careful preparation. The file or folder should be (re)organized specifically for the course or job being applied for – highlighting exam certificates, a photo from work experience along with the employer's report, something striking and relevant about their spare time interests, Saturday job, a particular talent or experience, and so on. The folder needs to be easy to handle, and everything in it needs to be clear and, if necessary, well-labelled. A 'practice run' is essential to make sure the folder works and that the pupil is comfortable and fluent when using it.

(Some young people get into their local paper in connection with their disfigurement, e.g. 'Brave Rosemary meets Simon Weston', with a press photo and caption explaining their burns and their visit from the now famous ex-soldier burnt in the Falklands. These kind of 'stories' can be included in a presentation folder but care and thought are required as they may invoke pity or awe, which is inappropriate to the interview situation.)

'Is there anything you would like to ask us?'

A typical question might be, 'What kinds of jobs and courses do the students go on to do after they've completed this certificate?' An applicant who had a port wine stain and was trying for a place on a hairdressing course, asked first if the students got to attend specialist courses run by the manufacturers of the various products. Then she asked, 'Have you ever had anyone on this course with a disability or a difference like a birthmark?' (she had practised the question to achieve a purely interested tone with no 'axe to grind'). The answer was no and the applicant was successful.

The biggest step

A school leaver who gets a job with a small firm who do their training in-house will meet and get to know a few new people. Anything else means meeting many more: new teachers, tutors or trainers, supervisors and managers, but also a whole new peer

Table 10.2 Where to get help or advice

Organization	What they can offer	Contact name	Contact details	Other points
Connexions (still Careers Office/Youth Advisory Service in some areas)	Personal adviser to help get established in training or work. Can also help with other problems – housing, health, etc.	Personal adviser ... Careers adviser ... Special needs careers adviser ...		
Local colleges/ sixth form centres (list them all)	Broad categories of courses offered	Learning support co-ordinator or equivalent ... (for each institution)		
Job centre	Job vacancies and access to special schemes	Disability employment adviser or DEA ...		
Changing Faces	Social aspects of looking different – advice and support		020 7706 4232 1 & 2 Junction Mews, London W2 1PN info@changing faces.co.uk	Covers whole of Britain 9 to 5 Mon to Fri
Disability Rights Commission – helpline	Advises individuals who may have been discriminated against. Advises organizations how to operate more fairly		08457 622633 / 08457 622 644 DRC Helpline, Freepost MID 02164 Stratford upon Avon CV37 9BR www.drc-gb.org	Covers England, Scotland and Wales 8 to 8 Mon to Fri

group or colleagues – most of these people will have little or no experience of having a student, trainee or colleague who has a disfigurement. Hopefully school will have equipped the school leaver with the social skills and strategies – with the *expertise* – they will need to enable these new people to get to know them for the person they are, as well as what they look like (see Chapters 2 and 7).

But school leavers with disfigurements do face very real social challenges as they move out into the wider world. A list of potentially useful contacts can help a school leaver to manage what they can for themselves and get help or advice when they need to. A 'localized' contact page along the lines outlined in Table 10.2 can be added to the kind of 'useful information for school leavers' which many LEAs and/or Connexions or careers services already produce. Create your own version of Table 10.2 with all local contact details completed, or make this a task for school leavers themselves (but check carefully that they have got it all right).

Disability Rights Commission

Under the Disability Discrimination Act 1995, many legal rights and obligations affecting disabled people including people with severe disfigurements are now in force – concerning employment, access to services, education, transport and housing. The Disability Rights Commission is an independent body established by Act of Parliament to eliminate discrimination against disabled people and promote equality of opportunity.

The DRC can help individuals who have disabilities or disfigurements and think they may have been discriminated against. It can also help organizations to adopt policies and practices which treat everyone more fairly.

Chapter 11

Medical needs, special educational needs and related issues

It can be tempting to find out a lot about the condition or injury which affects a pupil in school. The internet, medical dictionaries, information services provided by support groups . . . Questions can proliferate: What is it? How do you pronounce that name? What does that name mean? Is it very rare? What caused it? Is it catching? What makes the bones/skin grow like that? Does it hurt? What's the treatment? Can it be cured? Can it be improved? Does it deteriorate? Will it go away? What about (more) plastic surgery? Does it affect people in other ways? Information is so important . . .

There isn't space here to provide comprehensive information about disfiguring injuries, illnesses and conditions, and it would duplicate much that is available elsewhere. Instead, we offer:

- guidelines to help keep the individual child or young person in focus (see the checklist and notes on special educational needs below)
- some background regarding the way various disfiguring injuries and conditions affect the people who have them and the implications for their school education

These will help school staff ensure that their pupil receives the education they need to realize their potential both educationally and socially.

Figure 11.1 'Several of the other children asked about Casey's cream. As the plunger keeps it hygienic we decided they could all have a little squirt. It was fun and everyone seemed less bothered about Casey's eczema after that.'

Checklist for obtaining information

- Who is this child? What has happened to her face?
- How does this affect her? (Speech? Breathing? Swallowing? Hearing? Sight? Sensitivity to heat or cold?) How does she manage?
- Is her condition stable or will it/could it alter? Gradually or suddenly?
- Does she have any special medical needs related to this disfigurement?
- Does she have any special educational needs (which may or may not be related to the injury or condition that affects her appearance)?
- Is she having/going to have any treatment?
- How does/will this affect her? (Many health professionals and parents report a period of 'regression', particularly for younger children, following traumatic or invasive treatments such as surgery, or time in hospital. A pupil may be less able, less independent, or more needy, for a while.)
- If school attendance may be affected, how can teachers, parents and health professionals work together to ensure the child's continued sense of belonging in the school, and how will the continuity of her education be safeguarded?
- How is she likely to be affected longer term?
- How does she get on socially – with strangers? with adults? with other children or young people?

Special educational needs

A child with a disfiguring injury, illness or condition may not have any special educational needs. Or some needs may have been recognized while others have gone unnoticed:

> In primary school visual impairment problems [were] addressed . . . [but] the main personal/emotional problems had not been addressed.[1]

There is some evidence that teachers can find it harder to assess the ability of children with facial disfigurements, overestimating the ability of less able children and underestimating the ability of more able children.[2]

A child can be seriously adversely affected by not having a special educational need recognized in good time. They may already be stressed by their experience of the injury, illness or condition that affects the way they look, or by its medical treatment. They may have fewer personal resources to call upon to overcome difficulties which may arise from time to time at school. In some cases the additional stress of difficulties at school may cause a child's condition to worsen.

If a pupil's health, learning or behaviour worsens the school should consider whether the child has a special educational need and be ready to undertake an assessment if appropriate.

Dangerous data

Children can also be adversely affected by being thought to have special educational needs which they do not in fact have. For example, some conditions, particularly conditions that have a genetic component, are often described as having have associated learning difficulties.

Educational professionals must take especial care to keep the focus on the individual pupil and not give undue weight to general medical information.

- Associations between disfiguring conditions and learning difficulties are invariably statistical – for example, 40–60 per cent of children with neurofibromatosis have specific learning difficulties.[3] What this means, of course, is that 60–40 per cent of children with this condition who have been assessed for specific learning difficulties were found not to be affected.
- The assessments upon which the statistics are based may themselves have been flawed. In some cases samples are very small. In others the data is very old and derived from approaches no longer in use, or for which adequate records have not been kept.
- When cognitive ability is assessed verbally, the ability of children with cranio-facial conditions (who often have delayed speech – see below) is very difficult to evaluate accurately. If non-verbal methods are used to assess cognitive ability, for children whose hands or limbs are affected (which is the case in a number of cranio-facial conditions) accurate assessment of ability is again jeopardized.
- Eyesight difficulties associated with some cranio-facial conditions can be difficult to diagnose accurately, particularly in very young or speech-delayed children. But without good corrected vision it can be painfully hard for a child to engage in learning activities or participate properly in cognitive assessments.
- Any child's capacity to function well educationally is strongly influenced by other people's expectations of them.[4] The way other people – particularly teachers – 'see' children with disfigurements may adversely affect their self-esteem and motivation.

'Older-appearing' children

The age and maturity of children *as perceived by others* also influences the recognition of their abilities. It can be difficult to judge the age of an infant or child who has a facial disfigurement. Many are seen as older than they actually are. This leads to their being expected to be capable of *more* behaviours than are expected of other youngsters of their age. 'Older-appearing' infants and children then receive global evaluations indicating that they are viewed as less competent *because* they cannot meet the higher expectations for specific developmental abilities that adults seem to hold for them.[5]

All this leaves teachers and other educational professionals with a very special and delicate task regarding any pupil who is visibly different, particularly when the face and/or hands are affected. Observations of their pupil at work and at play must be ongoing, objective, sensitive, imaginative and accurate. Feedback to the child must be appreciative, motivating and respectful.

If a pupil requires ongoing or periodic medical care or management in school

Some pupils have conditions, injuries or illnesses which, if not well managed, can limit their access to education, as well as affecting their health and well-being and giving rise to emotional and behavioural problems. These pupils are regarded as having medical needs. Health Authorities, Local Education Authorities, and governing bodies should work together to ensure that pupils with medical needs and local staff have effective support in schools.

A pupil may fall into this category particularly if they have burn injuries, a serious skin condition, a haemangioma, or if they have had recent surgery (but this is not an exhaustive list). The management of their medical needs in school can involve simple practical considerations regarding the immediate environment. For example, heat may be both uncomfortable and detrimental for a pupil with severe eczema, or a haemangioma, or who is recovering from burns. In winter a child may need to sit away from radiators to prevent them becoming distracted by physical discomfort; in summer they may need a fan to help keep them cool enough to be able to concentrate on lesson activities.

> It rained all the time on the field trip. They wanted us to wear these plastic rainmacs but I couldn't stand the heat. I said I'd rather be wet and cool than dry and hot. Fortunately Mr Singh understood what I was on about.

The pupil's access to the full curriculum, particularly PE and swimming, will also be of concern. It may seem best to excuse a child from these activities, for instance because of the problem of reapplying treatments, pressure garments, etc. after the child has showered and dried off. However, it is also often the case that these activities are of great importance to a child who may have been physically constrained for long periods by their injuries or condition and who needs to recover or maintain physical tone, strength and mobility.

When a pupil has medical needs, it is helpful for a school to draw up a written health care plan involving the parents and relevant health care professionals. For practical guidance on meeting a child's medical needs in school, refer to *Circular 14/96* and *A good practice guide: supporting pupils with medical needs*, produced jointly by the Department for Education and Employment and the Department of Health. The circular clarifies the legal framework for the provision of medical care in schools. The guide covers the practical aspects of meeting a pupil's medical needs, including responsibilities, the development of policies and procedures within your school, dealing with medicines, and drawing up a pupil's health care plan.

Regarding the role of staff in school, there is no legal or contractual duty on teachers to administer medication; this is a voluntary role. However, support staff may have specific duties to provide medical assistance as part of their contract. Health Authorities normally designate a medical officer with specific responsibility for children with special educational needs (SEN) and NHS trusts, usually through the School Health Service (SHS), may provide advice and training to school staff and, in some cases, may provide specialist support.

Background notes for school staff when a pupil has a disfiguring injury, illness or condition

Birth and early development

There are many named conditions (most of which are very rare) where the bones, muscles and other tissues and organs of the head and face do not develop in the usual way. A relatively frequently occurring example is cleft lip and palate (one in 600 live births). Many people will have encountered a pupil (or a colleague) with this condition – a child with a unilateral cleft may have a small scar from their upper lip to their nose, and their nose may be asymmetrical. This, however, is a *repaired* cleft lip. The child's cleft palate, which a cleft lip often but not always accompanies, is another story, largely hidden from view.

Being born with a cranio-facial condition has an enormous and prolonged impact on a child's physical and psychological development and well-being. From before birth (if an ultrasound scan shows a cleft or other cranio-facial anomaly, for instance) a specialist medical team (often at a specialist hospital far from home) will have become involved, including specialist nurses, psychologist, speech and language therapist, orthodontist and surgeon. Similarly, if a condition such as haemangioma (present at or soon after birth) affects an infant's head, face or neck, there will be medical issues.

Typically, the newborn's early years and their parents' early experiences of caring for them will be dominated by concerns over breathing and feeding. Later there are often concerns over hearing, and speech development.

A child with a condition affecting their face, head or throat may be or have been vulnerable in some or all of the following areas.

Breathing

Breathing may be restricted whenever the face or neck are affected. In cranio-facial conditions the airway may be restricted by the position of the tongue, or by the under-development of the bones of the jaw or face. A haemangioma, even if apparently small or located on the face only, may extend into the throat. Haemangiomas and lymph-angiomas can develop and change, presenting additional concerns. Babies and infants often have a tracheotomy ('trakky' for short) which is an operation to insert a 'breathing hole' into the windpipe (trachea) below the throat. The child's life then depends on their trakky being kept clear and their parents are taught to maintain the trakky in good condition. In some cases, it may be so hard for an infant or child to breathe that surgery to improve other functions cannot be undertaken.

Children with external burn injuries may also have injured the inside of their mouth, nose, throat and lungs, through inhaling hot air or smoke.

Feeding

Feeding can be a major challenge, too, either because the throat is restricted, as described above for an infant with a haemangioma or, as is often the case with a cleft lip and palate and some other cranio-facial conditions, because of the way the infant's mouth is affected. In order to feed, the baby must grip with the mouth and close off the nasal cavity to create a chamber of reduced pressure into which milk is drawn. When a suitable amount of milk has been taken into the mouth, a swallow is triggered – and all this must be achieved while continuing to breathe. Feeding can be stressful and exhausting, and takes much longer than for unaffected infants. In some cases an infant may have to be fed via a syringe, and sometimes a gastric tube is inserted surgically to enable an infant or small child to feed sufficiently. If a newborn is not to remain in hospital, the parents may have to learn to use special equipment and nutritional supplements or their baby will fail to thrive.

Speech

Speech is invariably affected for all sorts of reasons. If an infant is hospitalized for long periods, their social experiences and interactions will be quite different from an infant who is at home with a family. Any hearing impairment, temporary or permanent, will affect babbling and the acquisition of speech. If an infant's throat or breathing are affected, by a haemangioma for instance, or if they have a 'trakky', they may not make voice sounds at all. Delayed babbling and then delayed – perhaps seriously delayed – speech are also characteristic of infants with cranio-facial conditions.

Any variation in the jaw, lips, teeth, tongue, soft and hard palates or in the muscles and tissues at the back of the mouth or the top of the throat will seriously affect a child's ability to produce speech sounds. Children are highly motivated to communicate and can readily learn to combine simple signing, pointing at things, gestures, etc. with speech sounds – 'total communication' – to overcome their communication difficulties. Those around them, and especially at school, need to be imaginative and adaptable to maintain and develop the child's motivation to communicate.

Importantly, a cranio-facial condition that seriously affects the child's appearance may not unduly affect their speech, whereas a cleft which appears to be well-repaired externally can belie a seriously affected palate and pharynx.

Many children with clefts undergo complex surgery, often involving several operations, to increase their capacity to close off their nasal cavity when speaking, or to create or extend their hard palate or soft palate to enable them to articulate speech sounds more accurately. Most cleft repairs also involve serious, long-term orthodontic work. Outcomes can be very variable and children may be fitted with prosthetics to improve their speech. Children with clefts often sound hypernasal (air in the nose) and may find it hard to achieve certain vowel sounds. Other difficulties in managing speech production can lead to speech which sounds characteristically breathy or wet and may be quite indistinct. Or a child's speech may be 'almost normal':

> Pupil [has become an] 'elective mute' as he makes unusual sounds when saying 's' and 'sh'. [He] is teased so resorts to silence when asked questions by staff and pupils.[6]

For all this, most children are keen to communicate. School staff, in collaboration with the child's speech and language therapist, 'only' need to help and encourage them achieve the clearest, most intelligible speech that they can. It is particularly important for school staff to be very clear about what aspects of speech the child can be expected to improve with care and practice, and what aspects of their speech difficulties are outside their control. A child's efforts and achievements can then be properly noticed and appreciated, which will spur them on to keep trying.

Conversation is the most common context for talking. It involves taking turns, introducing, maintaining and switching topics, requesting and making clarifications, and listening. Conversation has an open-ended and speculative quality. Learning conversational skills involves learning to listen more and interrupt less, learning to *notice* the listeners' level of interest or participation, and learning to moderate voice tone, volume and style to the occasion. Eye-contact and body language are important components of conversation. For children with delayed speech, and for children who have more contact with adults such as health professionals and other specialists and carers than with peers, conversation can become a mystery.

Classroom talk is quite different from conversation. Typically, two-thirds of the 'turns' are taken by the teacher. Small group sessions which are teacher-led rather than teacher-dominated can help a child to practise a wider range of conversational skills. Practioners in classrooms who are not teachers, such as learning support assistants and nursery nurses, are often better than teachers at offering pupils more 'communicative space' in dialogue.[7]

Hearing

Hearing may be affected because some part of the ear is un- or differently-developed. Hearing aids may then be set into the bone of the skull, often with fairly good results. Children who wear hearing aids have, of course, a range of sound-related special needs in the classroom and around the school.

In other cases, hearing is affected (as in children with clefts for example) because of a much greater susceptibility to ear infections, due to differences in the position and function of the tissues of the mouth and throat. Grommets may be fitted. Hearing loss can be mild and intermittent – but even this can seriously affect a child's progress in school, particularly as it can be very hard for others – or even for the child – to know when hearing is good and when it is poor. In particular, when a child doesn't hear – and therefore 'ignores' – spoken questions or instructions which, a few days earlier, they seemed to be able to hear without difficulty, this can be misconstrued as inattentive, rude or mischievous behaviour. Over time, hearing loss can become more marked and more permanent.

Certain skin conditions occasionally affect hearing, if the skin in and around the ears is affected and especially if it becomes infected.

Eyesight

Eyesight can be affected by difficulties associated with the structure and function of the bone or other tissue near the eye. A haemangioma or a plexiform neurofibroma, for instance, near the eye may tend to close the eye.

If a cranio-facial condition affects the muscles around the eyeball, it can lead to difficulties with vision. This may be hard to identify and correct if language is delayed. In one case, a child who was so aimlessly inattentive at school that he was seen as having severe learning difficulties was eventually treated for extreme long-sightedness by being fitted with a pair of glasses. Within weeks his attentions levels and performance in class had been transformed.

A child with Moebius Syndrome or any other kind of facial paralysis may not be able to move their eyes as most of us do without having to think when we read. Another child, for example with albinism, may not be able to control their rapid lateral eye movements due to nystagmus.

In some cases the eyes are physically vulnerable due to the shape or position of the surrounding bone, or because of difficulties with the eyelids or tearducts. In other cases a child may see better when looking to the side than when looking straight ahead. This can make eye-contact problematic when communicating – again, especially if language is delayed. Even a 'slight squint' can have quite serious social implications because of its effect on making and experiencing eye-contact with others.

As with hearing, if a skin condition affects the skin around the eye or the eyelid, vision can be impaired.

Motor skills

Motor skills are affected whenever an illness, injury or condition affects hands or feet or other joints, or when the skin is affected.

Burns, other traumatic injuries and also illnesses such as meningitis can lead to loss of or damage to fingers or hands and there are several cranio-facial conditions where fingers may not have developed or separated in the usual way. These all have implications for fine motor skills. Surgery often helps but a child may take much longer to learn and carry out manual tasks – pulling up a zip or turning over a page, as well as holding a pencil or a knife and fork.

Children can appear more self-conscious about their hands – which they themselves can see all the time – than about their facial appearance:

> Jenny used to slip off her chair and curl up under the table. You couldn't get her to come out. The LSA commented once that it was to do with putting up her hand – she just couldn't bear to do this. We came up with the idea of coloured cards. All the children had a set of coloured cards in their trays. If someone had a birthday, they could choose which cards we went with that day. Instead of 'Put up your hand when – whatever –' I'd say, 'Hold up your red card'. Fortunately, it worked.

Skin

Skin conditions and scarring from burns or other surgery can restrict movement by making the skin too tight or too stiff or sore to move. If a hand is affected, holding a pen or pencil to write or draw may be very painful and a child may need to use a computer where keys can be tapped without the requirement to move fingers so much.

During recovery from surgery to the hands or from injuries such as burns, or if a skin condition affects movement, the child's physical well-being and educational progress at school require the involvement of their physiotherapists and/or occupational therapists.

Skin serves many vital functions – it keeps moisture in, and keeps everything else out, including infections. It grows as the person it covers grows. It is very flexible and can recover quickly from minor knocks and grazes. It is washable but it also looks after itself by means of oily secretions and replaces itself constantly so that it never 'wears out'. It helps manage body temperature by varying blood flow and perspiration. Skin is tactile and sensitive – the nerves in hair follicles on the skin are among the most sensitive nerves in our bodies.

Skin conditions are often extremely and permanently uncomfortable for the children and young people who have them, and can be 'socially aversive' as people often have a misguided but deep-seated fear of 'catching it'. Skin conditions which 'shed' can be very disconcerting for others. (It is, however, the child with the skin condition who is often at high risk of infection which their affected skin is unable to keep out.) Mobility and facial expression may be severely restricted. (See *Motor skills* above.) If feet are affected a child may need to use a wheelchair.

If a child takes medication to reduce itching or to enable them to sleep at night, they may be drowsy in class. But if they don't take medication and don't sleep well, discomfort and tiredness may prevent them from concentrating. As mentioned above, healing burn-scars and some skin conditions can make children very sensitive to heat.

Children whose skin is scarred often require surgery from time to time through out their growing years to 'release' tight scars called contractures, or to allow for growth. Any part of the body can be affected, including mouth and neck, armpits, and so forth.

Compliance with treatment

Compliance with medical treatments is a concern for children with certain conditions. During the long process of recovering from burn injuries, a child may be required to wear pressure garments and/or a plastic face-mask. The purpose is to reduce the blood supply and the temperature within the scar tissue, and to keep new scar tissue as 'flat' as possible. Children with skin conditions are often required to apply and re-apply emollient or other creams several times a day, or they may be 'wet wrapped' to maintain permanent lubrication of the skin. Some children comply fairly readily most of the time with their treatment requirements, while others resist and avoid, seemingly intent on harming themselves further.

Exercises prescribed by a physiotherapist for hand function, say, or by a speech and language therapist to achieve or maintain certain speech sounds, can also be very hard for some children to comply with.

Treatments can make children feel even more 'different' than they already are from their peers. Dabbing some E45 on everyone's nose, and the resultant laughter and interest can be helpful. A star-chart may be worth trying although this can seem to confirm the absence of any intrinsic value for the child in the treatment they are having. As a general rule, children are not helped by being criticized, warned or punished for non-compliance. They do better when instances of good compliance are recognized with quiet appreciation for the discomfort and inconvenience that the child is willing to tolerate.

When there are concerns about compliance, it is particularly important for school staff, parents or carers at home, and the medical team, to work together and ensure the child is not being subject to confusing or contradictory demands.

Balance

In general, children seem to do best when school staff are sensitive and imaginative regarding the physical and medical aspects of their injury or condition, while keeping the child's participation in and enjoyment of school activities, both academic and social, as the main focus. Good links with the health professionals involved in a pupil's treatment or care are very important – but school is well-placed to be a key component of a child's 'ordinary life' away from medical concerns.

The child or young person's medical needs must always be respected by all school staff. However, school staff and classmates have a crucial role in enabling a pupil to feel that their place at school is being 'kept warm' for them whenever their injury or condition keeps them away for a day or longer.

Resources

There are many organizations and support groups, and many books and other resources, concerned with illnesses, injuries and conditions that may affect appearance. Here are just a few whose approach most directly addresses the personal and social issues associated with being visibly different.

Information and advice

Changing Faces, 1 & 2 Junction Mews, London W2 1PN
Tel: 020 7706 4232 fax: 020 7706 4234 e-mail: info@changingfaces.co.uk website: www.changingfaces.co.uk
   Information and advice for managing the psychological and social concerns when someone has an injury, illness or condition that affect the way they look. Includes a school service. The children and young people's service includes a counselling and support service for parents, children and young people. There is also an adult service.

Contact a Family, 209–211 City Road, London EC1V 1JN
Tel: 0808 808 3555 (helpline)
   Information and advice for parents of children with any disability or a specific health condition. Information about national support groups.

Other resources for teachers

Atopic eczema – an activity pack for teachers.
National Eczema Society, Hill House, Highgate Hill, London N19 5NA
Tel: 020 7281 3553 or 0870 241 3604 (helpline) e-mail: helpline@eczema.org website: www.eczema.org

Children born with cleft lip and palate: The school years – Information for teachers, carers and parents.
Cleft Lip and Palate Association, 235–237 Finchley Road, London NW3 6LS
Tel: 020 7431 0033 e-mail: info@clapa.com website: www.clapa.com

Genes and you: Teaching about genetics from a human perspective by Gill Mullinar. A large binder full of information and teaching materials for use in KS4 science and secondary school PSHE lessons.
Genetics Interest Group, Unit 4D, Leeroy House, 436 Essex Road, London N1 3QP
Tel: 0207 704 3141 fax: 020 7359 1447

S.S.P.I.D.E.R. handbook (Symbol systems and peer interaction: Developing educational resources). A practical guide including games and activities, to improve interaction with classmates for children using communication aids.

Mrs Eileen Carter, The Wolfson Centre, Mecklenburgh Square, London, WC1N 2AP
Tel: 020 7730 website: www.kidscape.org.uk

A wide range of anti-bullying services and resources for schools is available from:
Kidscape, 2 Grosvenor Gardens, London, SW1W 0DH
Tel: 020 7730 3300 website: www.kidscape.org.uk

Drawing the real you. Resource for teachers of art to promote positive inclusive and enjoyable approaches to looking at and creating images of people.
Changing Faces, 1 & 2 Junction Mews, London W2 1PN
Tel: 020 7706 4232 fax: 020 7706 4234 e-mail: info@changingfaces co.uk website: www.changingfaces.co.uk

Make the difference. This video-based resource looks at what the major world belief systems tell us about disfigurement, disability and difference. It enables teachers to address this sensitive topic knowledgeably and effectively, and teaches inclusive ways of seeing and meeting each other. Available from *Changing Faces* (see details above).

Managing the future after burns. A series of booklets including information for teachers and parents, and for children and young people themselves. Available from *Changing Faces* (see details above).

Books for children and young people...

Showtime by Alex Clarke, published by *Changing Faces* (ISBN 1 900928 28 0) £3.95.
   In this simple, illustrated story Emma shows her burn scars to her classmates and answers their questions. Available from *Changing Faces* (see details above). Ages 4–8

Barney's head case by Lynn Markham, published by Mamoth (ISBN 0 74974 700 5) £3.95.
   Barney's head undergoes an unexpected change. Not only does he have to deal with his feeling about this, but with everyone else's reactions too. Ages 8–12

1   *Looking different, feeling good!* (ISBN 1 900928 16 7) £3.00
2   *What happened to you?* (ISBN 1 900928 17 5) £3.00
3   *Do looks count?* (ISBN 1 900928 18 3) £3.00
4   *You're in charge!* (ISBN 1 900928 19 1) £3.00
   Young people who have got to grips with other people's annoying reactions share what they know and help the reader to develop effective strategies of their own. Four workbooks in colour. Available from *Changing Faces* (see details above). Ages 10–14

Face by Benjamin Zephaniah. Published by Bloomsbury (ISBN 0 7475 4145 X) £4.99.
   A fast-talking, fast-action story in which life deals Martin an unexpected blow. How will his friends and his girlfriend react to him now that his face has changed forever? Age 12+

Mortal Engines by Philip Reeve. Published by Scholastic (ISBN 0 439979 43 9) £5.99.

A fantastic, futuristic story in which two ill-matched teenagers, one of them badly scarred, team up to solve a crime, settle an old score and survive. Their adventures take them into civilizations which have moved on in every way. Age 12+

...and for everyone

Changing faces: The challenge of disfigurement by James Partridge. Published by *Changing Faces* (ISBN 1 900928 12 4) £6.00.

A straightforward personal account of the experience of fire, medical treatment, physical recovery and the development of a new social style to manage other people's reactions to a changed appearance. Available from *Changing Faces* (see details above).

Visibly different: Coping with disfigurement by Richard Lansdown, Nichola Rumsey, Eileen Bradbury, Tony Carr and James Partridge. Published by Butterworth Heinemann (ISBN 0 7506 3424 3) £22.50.

A wide-ranging, in-depth, but also very readable account of the psychological and social issues associated with disfigurement. Recommended reading for anyone involved in the medical, psychological or social care of children and families affected by disfigurement.

Stigma: Notes on the management of spoiled identity by Erving Goffman. Published by Penguin (ISBN 0 14 012475 6) £7.99.

An exploration of perceptions, self-perceptions, and interrelationships when some people are 'different' and others are 'normal'.

Humpty Dumpty faces the future (ISBN 1 900928 27 2) £3.95.

A fun guide for everyone from 9 to 90! Available from *Changing Faces* (see details above).

Notes

Introduction

1 Based on OPCS (1988) *Report 1: The Prevalence of Disability among Adults*, Norwich: The Stationery Office.
2 Kish, V. and Lansdown, R. (2000) 'Meeting the psychosocial impact of facial disfigurement: Developing a clinical service for children and families', *Clinical Child Psychology and Psychiatry*, 5 (4): 497–512.
3 Lovegrove, E. (2002) 'Adolescents, appearance and anti-bullying strategies', Ph.D. Thesis, University of the West of England.
4 Partridge, J. (1994) *Changing Faces*, Second Edition, *Changing Faces*: London.
5 Goffman, E. (1968) *Stigma: Notes on the Management of Spoiled Identity*, London: Penguin.
6 Extensive research summarized in Kish and Lansdown (op. cit.).
7 Macgregor, F. (1990) 'Facial disfigurement: Problems and management of social interaction and implications for mental health', *Aesthetic Plastic Surgery*, 14 (4).
8 Ibid.
9 Macgregor, F. (1970) quoted in M.J. Hughes (1998) *The Social Consequences of Facial Disfigurement*, Aldershot: Ashgate.
10 Richardson (1970) quoted in R. Bull and N. Rumsey (1988) *The Social Psychology of Facial Appearance*, New York: Springer-Verlag, New York, Inc.
11 Kleck and Strenata (1980) quoted in R. Bull and N. Rumsey (1988) *The Social Psychology of Facial Appearance*, New York: Springer-Verlag, New York, Inc.
12 Speltz *et al.* (1993) quoted in R. Lansdown, N. Rumsey, E. Bradbury, T. Carr and J. Partridge (1997) *Visibly Different* Oxford: Butterworth Heinemann, p. 117.
13 Murray, P. (2002) *Hello! Are you Listening?* York: Joseph Rowntree Foundation.
14 Lovegrove (op. cit.).
15 Hughes, M.J. (1998) *The Social Consequences of Facial Disfigurement*, Ashgate, p. 3.
16 Foan, G., in an email from Cleft Lip and Palate Association (CLAPA), Sussex, 30 December 2002.
17 Goffman (op. cit.), p. 24.
18 Rubin, K.H. and Wilkinson, M. (1995) 'Peer rejection and social isolation in childhood', in R. Eder (ed.) *Craniofacial Anomalies: Psychological Perspectives*, New York: Springer-Verlag, p. 168.
19 The Warnock Report (1978) *A Question of Life*, London: Department of Education and Science.
20 Disability Rights Commission (2002) *A Guide for Schools*, London: Disability Rights Commission.
21 Ibid.
22 Kish and Lansdown (op. cit.).
23 Rogers, C. (2002) 'Mothering (fathering) children with special educational needs', working Ph.D. Thesis, University of Essex.
24 Young, I.M. (2000) *Inclusion and Democracy*, Oxford: Oxford University Press.
25 Murray (op. cit.).

I Our beliefs and feelings about disfigurement

1 Lansdown *et al.* (op. cit.).
2 Rumsey, Bishop and Shaw (1997) 'Historical and anthropological perspectives on appearance', in Lansdown *et al.* (op. cit.), pp. 98–9.
3 Research findings at Bowling Green State University, Ohio, USA. Reported in the *Guardian*, 14 August 2001.
4 Research findings summarized in *The Full Picture* (1996) London: *Changing Faces*.
5 Lay, G. (1998) *Seeking signs and missing wonders*, Monarch Publications.
6 Langlois, J.H. (1995) 'The origins and functions of appearance-based stereotypes', in R. Eder (ed.) *Craniofacial Anomalies: Psychological Perspectives*, New York: Springer-Verlag.
7 Findings summarized in *Facing Disfigurement with Confidence* (2001) London: *Changing Faces*.
8 Macgregor (1970) (op. cit.).
9 During a pupil's SEM assessment the school doctor made an appointment for the boy to be seen by an eye specialist. The boy's mother protested vehemently: 'Why can't they just accept him as he is? Do they really want him to have his eye out – surgery is a risky thing – and have a glass eye, just to look nice for them?'
10 Murray (op. cit.).
11 Rubin and Wilkinson (op. cit.).
12 Based on 'Family functioning' in Lansdown *et al.* (op. cit.), p. 168.
13 Rubin and Wilkinson (op. cit.).
14 Rogers (op. cit.).
15 Crocker *et al.* (1971) described in Lansdown *et al.* (op. cit.), p. 127.

2 Having something to say

1 Kleck and Strenta (op. cit.).
2 Ibid.
3 Bronfenbrenner, U. (1979) *The Ecology of Human Development*, Cambridge, Mass.: Harvard University Press.
4 Article in *New Nation*, 18 November 2000, p. 2.
5 How idealistic or ironic do you think this is? See Chapter 4, *Creating Inclusive School Communities*.
6 Partridge (op. cit.), p. 88.
7 Ibid., pp. 64–5.
8 Partidge (op. cit.).
9 Martin, D. (2000) *Teaching Children with Speech and Language Difficulties*, London: David Fulton Publishers.
10 Bull, R. and Rumsey, N. (1988) *The Social Psychology of Facial Appearance*, New York: Springer-Verlag, New York, Inc.
11 Martin (op. cit.).
12 Ibid., p. 14.
13 Murray (op. cit.).

3 A new pupil or a pupil returning from hospital

1 Richardson (op. cit.).
2 Ibid. For all ages of infants and children, in all kinds of experiments, the infants and children were not so interested in 'unattractive' of 'scrambled' faces. Physical attractiveness had an 'incentive value' for the infants and children looking at a wide variety of faces.
3 'The most successful strategy is the one that works best for the individual at the time.' Lansdown *et al.* (op. cit.), p. 184.
4 Rubin and Wilkinson (op. cit.).
5 Vandell, D.L. and George, L.B. (1981) 'Social interaction in hearing and deaf pre-schoolers: Successes and failures in initiations', *Child Development*, 52 (2): 627–35.

6 Bull and Rumsey (op. cit.).
7 The legality or otherwise of this under the Disability Discrimination Act has not been followed up.
8 Richardson (1970) quoted in Bull and Rumsey (op. cit.).
9 Kish and Lansdown (op. cit.).

4 Creating inclusive school communities

1 Murray (op. cit.).
2 See various sociometric studies summarized and further examined in Solano, C.H. (1986) 'People without friends: Loneliness and its alternatives', in V.J. Derlega and B.A. Winstead (eds) *Friendship and Social Interaction*, New York: Springer-Verlag.
3 Asher (1978) quoted in Solano, ibid.
4 Cited by Bell (1981) in Solano, ibid.
5 Ibid.
6 Rubin and Wilkinson (op. cit.), p. 163.
7 Buss (1986) quoted in Rubin and Wilkinson (op. cit.).
8 Various research summarized in Solano (op. cit.).
9 Children were much more likely to explore a strange environment with a friend than when alone. Schwartz, quoted in Solano (op. cit.).
10 Initiating and maintaining a friendship is a task accomplishment and gives rise to a higher or more successful social status. Harre, quoted in Solano (op. cit.).
11 Ibid.
12 Tiggemanne, Gardiner and Slater (2000) '"I would rather be size 10 than have straight As": A focus group study of adolescent girls' wish to be thinner', *Journal of Adolescence*, 23 (6).

5 Teasing, name-calling, ostracism and bullying

1 Dawkins, quoted in Lovegrove (op. cit), pate 177 – the figures for children severely bullied at school were 30 per cent of visibly different pupils and 14 per cent of pupils who had a medical condition which did not affect their appearance.
2 Lovegrove (op. cit.).
3 Marr, N. and Field, T. (2001) *Bullycide*, Didcot: Success Unlimited, p. 146.
4 Ibid., p. 146.
5 Lovegrove (op. cit.).
6 Schwartz *et al.* in Stevens, V., Van Oost, P. and de Bourdeaudhuij, I. (2000) 'The effects of an anti-bullying intervention programme on peers' attitude sand behaviour', *Journal of Adolescence*, 23 (1): 31.
7 Stevens *et al.*, ibid.
8 Cacioppo *et al.* in Lovegrove (op. cit.), p. 160.
9 Lovegrove (op. cit.) p. 162.
10 Smith and Sharp, quoted in Lovegrove (op. cit.).
11 Tiggemanne *et al.* (op. cit.).
12 Lovegrove (op. cit.).
13 Ibid., pp. 84–5.
14 Ibid., p. 88.
15 Ibid., Chapter 11.
16 Bryan, J.H. (1970) 'Children's reactions to helpers: Their money isn't where their mouths are', in J. Macaulay and L. Berkowitz (eds) *Altruism and Helping Behaviour*, London: Academic Press.
17 The video used in the research, Stevens and van Oost, 1994, is no longer available. Useful alternative resources are given at www.teachernet.gov.uk/bullying
18 Rubin and Wilkinson (op. cit.) pp. 164–5.

6 Self-esteem

1 Bull and Rumsey (op. cit.).
2 Lovegrove (op. cit.), abstract.
3 Ibid., p. 17.
4 Kish and Lansdown (op. cit.).
5 Lovegrove (op. cit.).
6 Lansdown *et al.* (op. cit.), p. 126.
7 *Looking Different, Feeling Good?, What Happened to You?, Do Looks Count?, You're in Charge!* Four workbooks published by *Changing Faces*.

7 Social skills for life

1 Rubin and Wilkinson (op. cit.).
2 Ibid.
3 C. Shipster, Speech and Language Therapist and cranio-facial specialist, Great Ormond Street Hospital, conference presentation at the Institute of Child Health, London, 3 February 2003.
4 Guralnick and Paul-Brown (1980), quoted by Rubin and Wilkinson (op. cit.).
5 Various research summarized in Kish and Lansdown (op. cit.).
6 Coles-Gale, B. (2001) 'A study to identify the factors that are associated with resilience in individuals with a facial disfigurement', internal report for University of Leeds/*Changing Faces*.
7 Ibid.
8 Rumsey *et al.* (op. cit.).
9 Feedback forms from two-day workshops run at *Changing Faces* in 2002.
10 R. Eder (ed.) *Craniofacial Anomalies: Psychological Perspectives*, New York: Springer-Verlag.
11 Murray (op. cit.) p. 28.
12 Goffman (op. cit.) pp. 29–30, including quotes from his earlier writing, *Alienation from Interaction in Human Relations*.
13 Byrne, quoted in Solano (op. cit.).
14 Murray (op. cit.) p. 27.

8 Self-perception and self-expression

1 Baker, *Out on a Limb*, quoted in Goffman (op. cit.).
2 James, H. and French, D. (2002) 'Plenty to declare', *Nursery World*, July.
3 Terdal, Jackson and Garner (1976), quoted in Rubin and Wilkinson (op. cit.).
4 Research summarized in Lovegrove (op. cit.).
5 Ibid.

9 Looking anew at a pupil's situation

1 Sylvia, K. and Lunt, I. (1982) *Child Development*, Oxford: Basil Blackwell.
2 With kind permission of Ryan and his mother, Gill Foan, of Sussex CLAPA.
3 Tom's brilliant speech first appeared in the *Changing Faces*, newsletter, April 2001.

10 Thinking about careers

1 Lansdown *et al.* (op. cit.).

11 Medical needs, special educational needs and related issues

1 O'Dell, L. and Prior, J. (2002) *Changing Faces: User Evaluation Survey*, preliminary report 17 July (internal document).
2 Bull and Rumsey (op. cit.), Chapter 7.